C000318995

No Abi

Bernard Thorogood

NO ABIDING CITY

*Change and Changelessness
in the Church*

SCM PRESS LTD

Cataloguing in Publication Data Available

334 01154 X

First published 1989
by SCM Press Ltd
26–30 Tottenham Road, London N1 4BZ

Typeset by J&L Composition Ltd, Filey, Yorks
and printed in Great Britain by
Richard Clay Ltd, Bungay, Suffolk

Contents

Introduction

One of the major questions that overshadows ecumenical progress is to do with the possibility of change, change in theology, in credal formulae, in the institutions of Christianity, in worship. Many Christians emphasize the large unchanging element, all that is set for ever. Others see very little that is unchanging and therefore feel free to develop new ways of thought, expression and action.

I have tried to explore this divide. I can only do it from within one tradition of church worship, that of the Reformed family. That is my bias. I do not see change as an enemy to be resisted but as the necessary risk entailed in all faithful pilgrimage. So my plea is for greater understanding and acceptance of change in all parts of the church of God, not that we have a guarantee that change means progress but that unchangeability belongs to God and not to any work of human minds and hands.

I am grateful to colleagues who share burdens and so make writing a possibility in a busy timetable, and to Jean Rolls whose unchanging readiness to cope with my scripts threatens to deny my thesis.

1

Peter's Toe

No doubt the approach to St Peter's in Rome was
designed to impress, and it does. The ceremonial avenue
and then the colonnaded piazza introduce us to vast
dimensions with elaborate architectural motifs. Then
the wide steps lead our eyes to the façade and, I must
confess, to some anticlimax. Although the broad front
has a variety of heavy features and is topped with
statues, there is a flatness about the façade which
reminds me of a palazzo rather than a church. Perhaps
the front view is not the best, and more exciting per-
spectives are from corners of the Vatican museum and
the gardens. The dome is tremendous, but I reveal my
insularity in thinking that the three rows of oculi are too
fussy, and is it possible that the lantern, an awkward
mixture of styles, is a little reminiscent of a crown roast?
For size and majesty it takes all the prizes, but comes a
poor second to St Paul's for sweet harmony in stone.

Inside there is a light and colour and a murmur that
fills the enormous space. Marble and gold, statues
perched over capitals, a dozen chapels with concurrent
masses, oversized memorials of popes, the gleaming
folds and forms of the Pieta, the barbaric columns of the
baldacchino and the constant stream of visitors with
chanting guides, all this moves us to wonder at the
audacity, skill and wealth of the builders. The guide
ushers the party beside the column near the altar where

the ancient bronze statue of Peter is seated. Many stroke
or kiss the extended right foot. The statue came from
the earlier basilica and is seven hundred years old, give
or take a few. Over these centuries so many thousands
have kissed Peter's toe that the metal has been worn to a
sliver. Peter has looked at them all. The frail elderly, the
black wrapped widows who always seem to be five feet
one, the soldiers off duty, the denim clad teenagers
with carefully frayed edges, all these follow the Victorian
tourists rejoicing in the conversion of John Henry
Newman, the aristocrats on the grand tour, European
royalty in carefully managed convoys, the armies of
Napoleon, the passionate cassocks of the counter-
Reformation, back to old Roman fishermen and tribes-
men from the unimaginable forests of eastern Europe.
All have touched that toe. There could hardly be a more
powerful reminder of the continuity of faith across the
ages and the nations.

Rome is indeed full of such reminders both in stone
and in flesh. Its great churches do not hold much appeal
for those spirits that crave simplicity, but they testify
nevertheless to the devotion of thousands who gave
their best in craftsmanship and art. Their building was
a witness to faith even though competitive passions
sometimes directed the height of the cupola. The people,
too, are often testimonies to the tradition, walking
ancient streets to ancient dark doors for early morning
mass. Coming towards you, around the street corner is
a mediaeval face above the black cassock. All continuity
is personalized in the pope, for all over Rome it is the
reigning pope's name that is celebrated on the great
monuments as patron of their restoration. In the piazza
outside St Peter's, when the pope gives a public blessing, there is a huge crowd decanted from a regiment of
coaches which bursts into long applause and cheers

when the pope appears, in a spirit of adulation which seems far removed from the Gospels but testifies, in this computer age, to the influence of Peter's toe.

The question that presses is whether continuity is essential to Christian faith, and what sort of continuity. There is an eternal dimension to faith, for it is a relation to the eternal God who surrounds historical time as the air surrounds a bird in flight. The temptation and the risk is to transmit that eternity to the creations of our minds and our hands, to our philosophies and our institutions. We tend to prescribe the for-ever-and-ever quality of Christ to the consequences of Christ in our human history. So we freeze the incarnation, building a changelessness of the mind in all parts of the church. For this is not just a Catholic and Orthodox problem; it touches us all. Protestants too have tried to eternalize their cities, whether Canterbury or Geneva, because we all see in our favourite icons a timeless face of Christ. We build eternal cities. Yet that is a contradiction, for the cities we know are always changing and are only butterflies on the face of the cosmos. Rome is not eternal. It is only three thousand years old with only two thousand years of Christian history, due to change out of all recognition in another millenium.

Those who kiss Peter's toe today are very different from their predecessors in the Middle Ages. The whole realm of angels and demons has fled from consciousness. The threat of hell, the trauma of purgatory and the romantic vision of heaven, all that which occupied such a central place in a mediaeval theology is now on the periphery. Horizons have widened immeasurably, with a knowledge of the way the world works which places the schoolchild today in a position of greater power than many savants of the past. Our cities change, as the scaffolding indicates and the musak intrudes and the fast food containers litter the streets. So is faith the same? What do we mean when we ask such a question, for who can compare one person's faith with another's? We can say that the object of faith is unchanging but it is not within our scope of measurement to judge the human response. Yet there is continuity in that response. Radical Protestants have been a little too ready to regard our response to Christ as a clean sheet on which to write whatever is inspired in each one of us.

For within all religions there is a profound trust in continuity of human response to the divine calling and a longing to be part of a tremendous history. A large part of religion is what is customary. From the prayer wheels of Tibet to the muezzin of Mecca the worshipper does what the ancesters did, and deviation is not to be indulged. We find this reality within ourselves when we come across new religious movements. The study of them has become so professional that NRMs are now frequently referred to by the initials. Our confusion or distress is generated by such a novel approach to the unchanging word of God, by new scripts, new temples, new disciplines, new ethical precepts. We see this as a threat to the truth of the old which has become so well established in our hearts and minds. New means competition. Different means false. Thus we have an in-built tendency to ensure the unchangeability of our responses to God, which stems largely from fear. If the new is good and true, perhaps the old has been revealed as inadequate and that would unsettle the faith of many. Such fear is very general but is not based on any firm grip on reality, for the reality is change and no abiding city.

At first sight, such a claim does not seem to match our efforts to put faith into stone. Yet all religious faith, being a human response to a divine gift, is affected by the vast changes in human society over the centuries. Catholicism has changed. Once it was plain ethical teaching that usury was wrong and thus was considered unfit for Christians, though fit for Jews. Now the Vatican has its bank and plies the money market along with the bankers of Zurich. Once it was said that sexual pleasure was a device of Satan which should be avoided, with celibacy as the far better way. Now sexual pleasure within marriage is seen as one of the gifts of God's creation. Once the followers of other faiths were regarded as children of the devil who had no religious truth but only superstition. Now the pope goes to Assisi to pray alongside the representatives of Buddhism and Jewry and the Sikhs. Catholicism, however, does not find it easy to admit that great changes take place. In Protestantism the greatest change has been to question the whole foundation of God's selection of the saved. We recognize how seminal a contribution Calvin made to such a wide range of Christian thought. But in stressing so firmly the initiative of God we now tend to see him downgrading the freedom of the human will, even to the extent of creating souls and at once consigning them to hell, a vision at far remove from the Abba, Father of the gospel. So today we in the Reformed tradition stress the calling of God rather than the selectivity of God, the opportunity for all rather than the privilege of the few. We are all in a learning process and I suspect that we are all still in the beginners' department, with far more to discover of the mystery of God than has been known. In Jesus Christ the full wonder of God was present in a human life, but we know only a little of that life and of its significance. Revelation does not end the mystery. It is like the drawing back of a curtain to let the sunlight stream into our room, showing up our colours and our dust, but never bringing us direct experience of the sun itself.

There are two major consequences of change in our religous response. One is to consider the place of the transcendent Lord in the human scene, and the other is to question the absolutism of Christian claims.

What does it mean to claim that the transcendent Lord of heaven and earth is present and known in our human experience? It is an unverifiable claim, a statement of faith, but is constantly made. Christians make it when they celebrate the eucharist or when they offer forgiveness in the name of Christ, or in his name pray for healing. Outside Christian faith many others make it when they specify a transcendent presence in the glory of a snowclad peak or a storm over the Dolomites or a blaze of spring flowers, brushed by an angel's wing. It is as though a window has been opened and we have seen, in a transitory way, the wonder of the creative God who holds the cosmos in his hand. This is the way which the incarnation in Jesus shows us plainly. The very ordinary features of human life, the pains and loneliness and pilgrimage become also a vision of glory and a statement of eternal truth.

Yet that opening of the window does not change the character of the window. This is the strange twist to our human response, to imagine that because the eternal has been glimpsed so our eyesight has grown eternal lenses. Our visible lives are still as transient as all created things, and our constructions of mind and of mortar are of the earth earthy, not of the heavenlies. Peter's toe may be for some a mental contact with the apostles, a physical hyphen of faith, but it remains a slab of bronze, no more and no less. I believe in the window-opening, that the eternal dimension of God is made known to us in our constricted lives, and that the beauties of art and nature are one sign of it, that human love is another, and that the sacraments, the forgiveness of sin and the healing of broken lives is a third. But I do not believe that any of the channels by which such vision comes is immaculate or inerrant or eternal. They are sufficient. God has so approached us that we can appreciate the pain-love of Christ and may know the wonder of his victory over death, we may taste the bread and wine and can witness the self-sacrifice of good people for noble purposes. We are not consigned to a one-dimensional universe. So the eternal realities become known to all those who have eyes to see and ears to hear, and, because Jesus calls us, we may know the inner character of the one who gives us life. It is a way offered to the world from beyond our space/time framework, but only known to us within that framework. The light of Christ spreads to all ages but has its focus firmly in one age of our history and one place of our geography. So we only glimpse the glory of God in the thought, custom, language, conduct, passion, colour, justice, courage, celebration of our passing existence. Incarnation is the way of the Lord.

When we have been made aware of some aspect of God's presence we tend to absolutize that glimpse. We claim the truth, and the truth is not relative. All parts of the Christian family thus claim particular importance for that understanding of God which has been written in their foundation documents or spoken by their founding father. It is easy to see this in Peter's toe. The great basilica and all it represents has made absolute one verse of scripture which states that 'on this rock I will build my church', regardless of the balance between that verse and the overall message of the New Testament, which tells us not to elevate one disciple above another and to honour above all the community of faith. But Protestants have frequently made similar claims about their special insights. A good example was

the Scottish Presbyterian insistence that a way of con-
ciliar church government was so valid, so biblical,
so necessary that no other form should be tolerated.
Echoes of that absolutism can still be heard in Scottish
debates on church unity when the dread word 'bishop'
is mentioned. More generally, Protestants in England
have given excessive value to one translation of the
Bible and one book of liturgical prayer. However splendid
the language and however solid a foundation stone of
the English church, these elements were of their time,
they were prepared at one phase of the development of
language and in one mode of piety. To build them into
an everlasting structure is like expecting Roman law to
be applied to the international banking of the city of
London. Fortunately, many excellent modern trans-
lations of the Bible have become available so that the gift
of Christ may be clothed in the language we use today.

One of the reasons for absolutizing our tradition is to
give us power. We can not only declare the truth but
admit others to the truth on our terms. This has been a
churchly temptation through the ages, and has sometimes turned the church of God into something very like
the mystery religions of the ancient world. If a person or
community actually holds the keys to salvation and
peace and health and wholeness, then godlike power is
in those hands. This renders a priest or a pope into an
emperor who can give the thumbs-up or thumbs-down
at the arena. Gone is the open-armed welcome of Christ
to all who carry heavy burdens, gone the universal
mercy of the cross, gone the acceptance of the un-
worthy. It was the first apostles who had to discover the
breadth of the appeal of Jesus, so that they could not
control the influx of strangers into the community, and
all those successors who have made exclusive claims
discover the same reality. We may define a narrow way

and the right teaching but Jesus escapes our fences, touching hearts and minds in a manner we cannot contain.

But what of conviction? Has not the greatest witnessing enthusiasm been shown by those who have a conviction that they hold the truth? The missionary martyrs through the ages have been single-minded people, sometimes narrow-minded people, utterly convinced that they have the word of salvation. This conviction has enabled them to endure lives of extraordinary hardship, to learn languages and commit them to writing, to travel amid danger and to face isolation from family and colleagues. Some of the greatest of these have rooted their conviction in their relationship with Jesus Christ and not in the formularies taught at the time by their particular order of Christian witness. I have stood by Robert Morrison's grave in Macao, recalling his pioneering of all Protestant missionary witness to China, and his passion for Christ which was far above his sense of authority in the church. He stands as one example of a life founded on conviction which nothing could shake, but a conviction about a person rather than an institution. What is the dividing line between conviction and fanaticism? I think it has to do with the learning process, the pilgrimage of faith. The fanatic has parcelled up his reality, tied it with the strings of orthodoxy, stamped it with divine authority and so has no discoveries to make. Christian conviction speaks of the wonder of the coming of God in Christ but knows how little is yet understood. We dare not absolutize these beginners' glimpses of the eternal grace which comes towards us in the pain of Christ.

There are dangers for us on either side of this argument. If we are inclined to profess the total adequacy of the tradition, the unlimited wisdom of the fathers, and the unquestioned righteousness of the institutional church then we stand in danger of creating an idol. We are close to the point of transferring the glory of God to the ambivalent glories of the human response to God. Some Christians stress the vital importance of learning the tradition, believing that back there at some point in history the fullness of understanding was given. So we have a *Summa Theologica*, a text which says it all. To have grasped that tradition and made it our own is then to become a master of the faith in our time. It is rather like schoolteachers who specialize in Latin and whose ambition is to produce good new teachers of Latin, a reproductive system which does little for students and much for specialists. So the traditionalist in religion may produce splendid expositions of the fathers or the Reformers which effectually place Jesus in ancient history. The system has taken over from the living Christ.

But for those who stress the continuing search for truth, there is also danger. The theme of pilgrimage has many depths of meaning for Christians: the following of the master's footsteps to the Via Dolorosa, the striving for moral excellence, the search for Christian unity, and the seeking first of all for God's kingdom to come on earth. All this has validity for many. But it can become a search for the Holy Grail, a running after a perfect state of being which is like a constantly retreating mirage in the desert. We can imagine that we are progressively building on the work of previous generations and so getting closer to the great experience of God's presence in the midst of our lives. But in fact we are no closer to God because of the long pilgrimage of the ages of faith. Herbert Butterfield, the historian, had a phrase that 'each generation is the same distance from barbarism', a daunting reminder of the fact of Auschwitz in our

Christian European culture. But we may also phrase it that 'each generation is the same distance from God'. We are no nearer to the ultimate reality than the Celtic saints whose lives now seem lost in the mist of the mountains; perhaps we are farther away. For the time line is not a progression into God or away from God. Each generation and each person has to make their own pilgrimage, the end of which is not evident to our eyes; the living Lord is equally close to each one. But are we not called to improve and reform and learn from mistakes? That must be so. We are thankful that the papacy learnt from the Reformation and never settled back into such corruption again, and that Protestants learnt to live in a plural society with tolerance for others. We can only be labelled fools if we refuse to learn from history. The risk is that we may imagine such learning will lead us to the kingdom, when the church will be the unspotted bride of Christ. In fact, we cannot make that progression because the sinfulness of Christians is not remedied by a historical learning process, it is much deeper than that, part of our mortality and our limitation and our distance from our own ideals. So while we learn, we err; while the pilgrimage goes on, we wander to right and left; and while we seek the kingdom in human societies, we corrupt even the beauty and the wisdom of our own culture. God's grace has not lifted us beyond this framework of uncertainty, but has brought his love towards us as we live within it.

We all need signs of that present, eternal, contemporary love in our lives, and perhaps Peter's toe is just one of them. There can only be thanksgiving that many Christians have been helped to know the Lord by such unremarkable pieces of metal or such simple sermons or such sentimental hymns or such ugly chapels. God has used so many means to tell us of his forgiving love, and each becomes precious to the believer. When we give to those means too great an importance, to label them with divinity or eternity or absolute truth, then we expose the Christian cause to schism and cynicism, for we are transposing into our particular language and claiming for our age the reality which is for all ages and languages without restraint.

Great cities look eternal. Westminster or the Capitol or the Kremlin say in stone that they abide for ever as symbols of the state. Yet they change. The Kremlin has seen one upheaval of authority in this century and could easily see another. Westminster has been reduced to a dwarf presence compared with its nineteenth-century power. So we also build into our religious shrines the appearance of immortality, and that stance is carried through into our liturgy, our ministry, our creeds. We need to distinguish much more carefully between the gift of God in Christ in which the eternal is revealed, and all the responses of believers through the ages which can impress us with their beauty and their strength but which are essentially part of the human process. We glimpse the eternal through such means and are grateful. But when Samuel Johnson's hymn proclaims

> Unharmed upon the eternal rock
> The eternal city stands

we shall know that this is no city we have ever seen, it is no institution we have ever served, nor is it any theology we have studied. It is always God's building prepared for us, beyond our architects and consti-tutional lawyers, beside which we are like children who in nursery rhymes sing of realities far beyond them and who have never touched more than the fringe of the robe of the Christ.

2

The Eternal Gospel

There is no element or dimension of Christianity more sure than this, that the gospel, the good news, is itself unchanging. Proclaimed across the centuries, this word remains the same. In every cultural context there remains but one gospel. And in all the variations of ecclesiology, and all the schools of theology, there is one bedrock, the gospel itself. Our confidence that this is so creates a powerful cement which binds believers to the tradition, so that however far apart they may be in their perceptions they are at one in trusting the good news of Christ. Is it so?

We have to ask about the nature of this unchanging gospel. A first answer may be that it is a series of historical events. Those events happened and their happening can never be changed. In the reign of Augustus, when Quirinius was Governor of Syria ... when Pilate was Procurator and Caiaphas High Priest ... when Felix was Governor and was succeeded by Porcius Festus. So the point in history is fixed for us, never to be amended. The place is fixed, that small tired strip of hill country set between the great powers, a Belgium of the Middle East. The personal genealogy is fixed, for although Matthew and Luke differ in many of the names, there can be no alteration of the actual persons in the family history. Such data may be considered totally set and unchanging, just as any documented slice of history.

Yet by itself that is not what we now have before us in the printed Gospels. There we have much more complicated documents. They were not written with the eyes or the resources of a modern historian who prizes objectivity and the meticulous checking of facts. They were stories of faith, written in faith in order to arouse faith. So they are very selective, giving much greater weight to the last week of the life of Jesus than to any other, holding up before us those facets of the ministry which demonstrate faith, and ignoring that whole span of the biography prior to the baptism in Jordan. But when we say that the Gospels were written in faith, what do we imply? We are suggesting that it was from a perception of the person of Christ that the church told the story of his life. Those who did not perceive him as the Christ did not tell the story. This is what turned the history from a negligible incident in a peripheral province of the Roman empire into the focal point of the human story.

We are now unable to reduce the written Gospels into simple historical narrative, for we have no tools with which to dissociate Jesus from the Christ. Various scholars have attempted this, but the result is largely conjecture. We cannot, for example, describe the birth of Jesus in a purely historical method because our knowledge of it comes through that faith of the early church which saw the data through the lens of the incarnation. I do not believe there is anything to be gained for the ordinary Christian pilgrim in this academic struggle to strip off the layers of faith from the narrative, but it is necessary to recognize the quality of the material we touch when we turn to the written Gospels.

Is that lens of faith unchanging also? When we know Jesus as the Christ, is our knowledge the same as that of

Irenaeus or Augustine? Or Peter? Our presumption usually is that there is identity of faith. I do not believe this can be sustained. For the actual content of faith is a composite of knowledge, interpretation, will, commitment and love which is highly personal. When Peter acknowledged Jesus as the Christ, that very name meant for Peter many things which entirely escape our minds today when we use the same word. Within that word lay whole strata of history and nationalism, persecution and longing which do not enter into our makeup. The apostles told the gospel story with that unique emphasis of eye witnesses who were utterly persuaded that they had seen the Christ of God, the chosen one, the lamb of God, the Son of the Father. Each of these phrases – and many others – represents an understanding of the historical event which we may approach and claim but which can never be precisely translated into our context.

If we speak of the eternal gospel or the unchanging gospel, we therefore claim that the Christ-event, seen through the faith experience of the apostolic church, is a permanent record for ever speaking of a profound reality to all humanity. Each reading and perception of that record will be different, for every human mind is unique. But there is sufficient unifying focus for this to be the bedrock of Christian continuity through the ages.

Yet this alone does not satisfy. If the gospel were no more than a record then, however permanent, it would take its place in the parade of great books along with the works of the disciples of Socrates. There are two other aspects which we need to note. The first is the quality of the event we know as the resurrection. The meaning of this for the first disciples was that the historical person with whom they had walked and talked was still with them, still effective to change human life, still touching the roots of social morality, still leading men and women to a new community reflecting the rule of God. In this way the historic event became continuous. We must be careful not to claim the wrong sort of continuity. The resurrection did not simply extend the incarnation and remove the reality of the cross. The break was a real one. Jesus died. That short period of physical life in which we see identity with our lives was over. The risen Christ and the exalted Christ mean for us that the coming of God into our world in Jesus was part of the eternal life of God. Thus the quality of love and truth and forgiveness which we see in the historical record is the 'for ever' in which our lives are set. The living God is God who was present with us in the years of the life of Jesus, and this is the ground of the claim that 'we have a man in heaven', that the scarred hands and wounded side of the man Jesus, and his tears in Gethsemane, are part of the meaning of the word 'God' for us. This continuity of the incarnate life with the eternal life of God is most vividly presented to us in the prologue to John's Gospel, where the Word is declared to be the power of creation, and again when John records the dialogue with some Jews about Abraham, with the astonishing words, 'In very truth I tell you, before Abraham was born, I am' (8.58 NEB). This is perhaps the most startling personal claim in the Gospels, since it means that Jesus was not only aware of the present identity between himself and the Father but also of the eternal dimension of his being. This is history recorded for us by faith, and there can be discussion on the accuracy of John's report. But here is the ground for saying that the incarnation is not just an historical episode, it also has current validity for every generation.

The second aspect of continuity is the presence of the Holy Spirit in the lives of the disciples. Jesus knew that there was a great deal he had been unable to teach the first disciples, much they had to learn if the kingdom-life was to be proclaimed to all. The promise of the Spirit was assurance of continuity. God would not leave those men and women to sort out their theology and morals by human wisdom alone – if it had been so, then surely Jesus would have chosen people for their wisdom. They would also have the companionship of the Spirit, the guide into the truth that God is always longing to give to the human heart. God is not only the transcendent creator and the incarnate word, but also the constant challenge of the holy to our corrupted lives and the constant bringer of healing gifts and the constant lover of wandering humanity.

Of course, this does not mean that there is always one way in which the Spirit is known. There are a thousand ways. There is one Spirit, as Paul frequently told his readers, but a diversity of gifts. There is thus no reason to suppose that the particular gifts which are right for one age and culture will be repeated in any exact way. Since the Spirit works through the minds and personalities of people, not by charms and nostrums, the kind of people we are shapes the activity of the one, eternal Spirit. So when we consider the unchanging character of the gospel of Christ, we add the unchanging influence of God the Holy Spirit received through the changing, uncertain, limited channel of human lives.

At every point the unchanging element is God, the changing element the human response. How then do we understand the eternal gospel? I would stress these elements.

God seeks to declare his will and purpose for the world. It is good news that the God who is beyond all our words and concepts does not leave us to climb up to him. He is self introducing. The Bible is filled with the

accounts of this activity, and supremely in the four
Gospels we meet God opening his heart to ordinary
people. The initiative is with him, so that the coming
into the world in Jesus Christ is crown and fulfilment of
an unchanging characteristic. I do not see any reason to
presume that the Bible contains the total record of God's
self-revealing in the world, but it is that record which
has moved us to faith, which is consistent, which shows
that the God who is beyond history also touches history
in a personal life. This stands in contrast to those
understandings of God (like the old mystery religions)
which regarded the human search as the prior action, so
that by learning and discipline men and women might
reach up to that plane of being where they begin to
know God. The gospel dynamic is the other way about.

The nature of the entry into the world is that of divine
humility. At every point where glory might be expected,
we find humility. The birth narrratives shout this surprise, the temptations in the wilderness affirm it, the
rejection of regal ambitions surprised many, the way to
the cross leaves no room for any doubt – that the
character of God known to us in Christ is of the
vulnerable, unprotected, often unnoticed one, the outsider. This is truly amazing. It would seem so much
closer to the reality of God the almighty that he would
be revealed in the majesty of human dignity and power.
That is usually the human presupposition. It is only on
deeper consideration that we see how this humility is
all-of-a-piece with the creation, for it is the character of
the creator to honour all that is made, to allow full
development, not to bully or compel but rather to move
humanity by the simplest word, to seek trust and to
offer service. To 'Lord-it' over creation would be to
belittle its quality and individuality, and so to deny the
possibility of growth into a free delight in being the

creation of one who loves us. This quality in God, the humble waiting, revealed in the incarnation, is at the heart of the gospel.

Within the story of Christ's ministry it is plain that there was a response to very basic needs of needy people. All have needs. But it was towards those aware of need that the response of love was made. The concern of Christ was not focussed on religious feelings but rather on the cry of the hungry and the sick; not that physical restoration was the great goal of his work but rather because the character of love is to reach out towards the critical need, whatever that may be. There is thus, in the eternal character of God, a recognition of the pains and tears of the human family, a readiness to meet them and, at the limit, to share them. God takes our struggles as genuine. Sickness and isolation are not imaginary, not to be wished away, nor to be ignored. The starving beggar at the gate is a real test of human character, not a myth organized by a public relations firm. The leper, the blind man, the epileptic, the mourners were people who knew their desperate need, and found in Jesus one who listened, cared and acted. So the nature of God is revealed.

Within the teaching of Jesus there is variety as we read the four Gospel records. There are the long set-piece addresses, the short, sharp sayings, the stories, the dialogues and the scriptural references. It is natural enough that different forms of the teaching circulated within the church in the period before the written accounts were widely available. What is very remarkable is that the essence of the teaching shines through so many diverse passages. The heart of it is the procla-mation of the reign of God, the manner in which God reigns, the way of life within his reign, the resistance to that reign, the joys of that reign for those who are despised by the world and the sorrows for those who think they have everything they need. The acts of healing were seen as part of that kingdom proclamation. The parables were pictures of what could not easily be projected in sermons. So the emphasis in the words of Jesus tells us that the purpose of God is that the human family might live in peace and sharing, in mutual support, in confidence and joy as children of the one father. That purpose was declared from the time of the ancient law and throughout the period of the prophets, but is affirmed by the very person of Jesus as well as his teaching.

The gospel stresses, without any uncertainty, that there is a struggle between good and evil, and that human life is an arena for that struggle. Whether we see the evil mainly in terms of human pride, selfishness, unbelief, ignorance and dishonesty, or in terms of the unsanctified social pressures which elevate status and denigrate service, or in terms of the unearthly powers which infect the human soul, the gospel offers a clear sign of resistance. The dark shadows are pushed away. The disordered mind is cleared. The guilt is forgiven. The leprous skin is healed. The stone is rolled away from the tomb. For the struggle is focussed on the one person who is dedicated to the holiness of God and in whom that holiness lives. He is the epitome of the eternal vigour of righteousness which the powers of evil must destroy if they are to dominate the human scene. The faithfulness of Jesus unto death tells us that evil in us, in the whole world, is not easily conquered.

There is, throughout the New Testament, a clear note of renewal and forgiveness. There was no period of history without a sign of human longing for peace with the divine forces which held sway in the universe. All ancient sacrifice was evidence for this. But with the coming of Christ a new door is opened and forgiveness is declared for those who approach God in humility and sorrow. This means that a renewed relationship with God is possible, not as a result of the splendour of our offerings, but because God has taken the initiative and drawn us to him in his own suffering. He has said in Christ, 'All you need is the heart of a child and the knowledge of your own sickness and a will directed towards the way of Christ – and I am with you.' Simplicity, directness, tears, infinite regret find their road to God is open, and new life a reality.

There is also an emphasis on the ultimate authority of God. Held back in all our human history, held, so to speak, in reserve, that authority is nevertheless the final arbiter of global destiny. So there is judgment, a deciding where we stand. We are not to be regarded as 'flies to wanton boys' who kill us for their sport, nor as numbers in a computer memory bank, but as those created and called to be part of the divine purpose, to live as part of God's life, lifted up by his energy and rescued by his love. That is the basis for the New Testament stress on judgment. The whole world is judged by what is beyond the world, the creation by the creator. So the values of the world with its petty rivalries and triumphs count for little on the ultimate scale. There the weights are labelled generosity, stead-fastness, humility and justice. Although we do not recognize that ultimate judgment in our newspapers, nor in Hansard, nor in the Annual Report of ICI, all our ephemera are yet answerable at the end. And the end is the victory of the creator's love. That is the testimony of dawn in the garden.

In describing so inadequately the permanent thrust of the gospel I have tried to avoid the use of the many technical terms which belong to the New Testament

period. These emphases I understand as aspects of
God. They are thus glimpses of the eternal declared to
us in our human environment. But even as I write, I
know that the very words I have used, and the selectivity
I have exercised, are part of the limitation of my own
culture and my own mind. We cannot evade that
limitation. The eternal gospel is focussed in that God-
revealing event which is the whole story of Jesus Christ,
but all our telling of it is partial just as our words and
images are limited.

The question has therefore to be pressed whether the
New Testament itself has this quality of limitation. I
believe it has. For while it is for ever the closest we
can get to Jesus, the one bedrock of our knowledge,
irreplaceable and life-sustaining, it is still framed in the
thought of an ancient civilization which we do not
share. For example, does the eternal gospel reside in the
stories of demon-possession, or in the high-priestly
pattern set down in the letter to the Hebrews? Are we
impelled to view the cross as substitutionary sacrifice? Is
Messiah/Christ the name which we must use? Christians
have given varied answers at this point, and there are
those who are confident that this written text is utterly
different from all others because the words are themselves given to us by the Holy Spirit, an eternal script.
It is surely true that the quality of the New Testament
writings testifies to a depth of spirituality very rarely
known in literature. But the difficulty experienced in the
early church, as it tried to limit the canon or list of
approved books, indicates that no decisive difference in
the nature of the books was then apparent. It was only
gradually that the present twenty-seven books received
general approval, and it was three hundred years after
the death of Jesus Christ before the canon we know was
written down. It is therefore extremely hard to believe

that these books were utterly distinctive because they were given verbally by the Spirit, and that no others were. There was, rather, a slowly developing awareness of the close links that these writings had with the apostles, an appreciation that they presented a cohesive account of Jesus Christ, and a thankfulness for the spiritual food they provided. Other books, like the Didache and the Apocalypse of Peter, fell into a secondary category. It therefore seems right to acknowledge that the writings of the New Testament are subject to human limitations, and that the lens through which we see Jesus is not guaranteed to be free from all distortion.

It is precisely here that we are always grateful for the multiple accounts of Jesus. If we had only one Gospel narrative, or several that were identical in approach, then we would be at the mercy of one human set of mind. But we have several views, each revealing a personal bias or interest. The Gospel of Matthew emphasizes the systematic teaching of Jesus in the pattern of a rabbi, fulfilling the historic Jewish faith, and setting the framework for a continuing church. The Fourth Gospel speaks more powerfully of the eternal Christ, the universal struggle between light and darkness, and the spiritual bonds between Jesus and the believers. Paul writing before either of those records, is strangely reticent about the biography of Jesus and concentrates our minds on the cruciality of the cross and resurrection as the key which offers humanity a way into a new creation. Such diverse emphases give to the New Testament a great richness and authenticity which could never be manufactured by a propaganda department.

But we study with some care to distinguish what is mainly a local, cultural or temporary word even in this apostolic witness. For example, the instructions of

Paul regarding women in church covering their heads and keeping silent, and the heavy emphasis on male seniority in the family now appears as a cultural bias and possibly even a personal prejudice, which we do not all accept as a word of divine authority. Indeed, in our day a man with a Mohican haircut would be far more disturbing in church than any hatless woman. Writing within a context of male dominance, it was a Christian word for Paul to stress the duty of generosity and kindness on the one side and humility and obedience on the other. To reproduce those arguments within our society today would not be life-enhancing or even sensible; it would be to insist on one stage of human development as the *status quo* for eternity. Similarly we may consider that some of the Gospel passages about dreams, voices, visions and angels are part of the temporary scene and do not have to be proclaimed as everlasting truth. This is a risky evaluation. We may simply place our own temporary standards as the criterion for judging an ancient text, and that would be to overturn the unique authority of the Bible. But it is an argument for a process of discrimination, that we should only claim eternal validity for that coming of God towards us in Christ, for the heart of God so revealed, for the gifts offered to us in Christ's obedience and love and victory, and for the supporting, healing presence of the Holy Spirit. It is there, in the God-revealing story, that eternal truth lives rather than in the interpretations of it that have taught us to formulate our faith. The human response to Christ is not the un-changing and unchangeable factor of our discipleship.

But this approach compels us to re-examine the meaning of scriptural authority. I am debtor to the Reformation tradition with its strong emphasis on *sola scriptura*, a tradition which lives in the basis of all the churches in the Reformed family today. In varying words these churches claim that the scriptures of the Old and New Testaments, interpreted under the guidance of the Holy Spirit, are 'sufficient' or 'ultimate' authority for the faith and conduct of all the people of God. It is a way of stating that these texts have a superior value for us than all others. This was the Reformation assertion in face of the mediaeval corruptions of the papacy and was, in large measure, the ground of the theological dispute. When Luther declared, 'Here I stand; I can do no other', he was standing on scripture, as contrasted with the declarations of popes and councils. Within the present ecumenical movement the same basis is frequently affirmed, for it is the area of Christian teaching which brings together the great majority of believers. I do not believe there is any other basis on which Christians can worship, serve, celebrate, and carry a cross together.

The critical phrase in most formulations is, 'interpreted under the guidance of the Holy Spirit'. This is one of the most precious and most abused of all theological statements. It is precious because we constantly have to interpret the text, and if human wisdom is the only tool then we open the way to the dominance of the intelligentsia. Precious also because the human questions we face today are so different from those of the apostolic age that interpretation is essential if we are to avoid an antiquarian literalism. But abused because of the individual licence assumed by many to read their personal likes and dislikes into the text, as when some extreme Protestants have regarded the scarlet woman in Revelation as a reference to the papacy. This has been a constant temptation of the more individualist Christian groups through the ages. We need an approach to the text that is ready to listen to the scholars, is humble about our own wisdom and is wholly devoted to the Christ who is lord also of scripture. The authority and continuing power of scripture in all branches of the Christian church is that here is a bedrock which cannot be wished away by centuries or quarrels or philosophies, but which is there for every reader at all times. Highly individualist interpretations will always need to be checked against the broad understanding of the church. How many Christians have interpreted the Apocalypse as providing a date for the Second Coming – a very popular occupation at some periods – only to find that the church as a body has no confidence in such prediction. It is precisely this uncertainty and irresponsibility which creeps into individual interpretation that strengthens a Catholic regime of centralized authority. I do not believe that is a way out of the problem. That central authority, too, may promote a strange interpretation. It is better to live with diversity which contains some error and some blessing than with a continuing and unarguable authority which itself may lead into a false emphasis. The scripture is for everyone. Once that book is open to all the people, no one can lock it up into an ecclesiastical system.

The eternal gospel is, at its heart, a revealing of the heart of God. It is a showing in the world of that loving, renewing, sustaining purpose which lies behind the whole cosmos, which we recognize in Jesus and which is proclaimed by the followers of Jesus in every age. It is a revealing of God which reaches us through human minds and human words and human institutions, all relying on God the Holy Spirit to lead them into truth, all conditional on human limitation, all to be received with thanksgiving, but none to be made absolute. God's gifts are for ever, because they are his own being shared in the world. Reception of those gifts is partial. That is why we walk in faith and hope.

3

The Gift of Salvation

Throughout the Christian epoch and across all the extraordinary diversity of human culture and within the unrepeatable individual, we claim the same gift of salvation. God has acted in Christ to bring salvation to the world. It is only if there is continuity here that Christianity makes any sense, for if the gift in Christ is a quite different matter in different centuries, then in effect there are different Christs. When the claim is made in the Epistle to the Hebrews that Jesus Christ is the same, yesterday, today and for ever, the writing is stating that the same authority, love, forgiveness and promise is available for every believer, unto the end of human history. The one initiative of God, itself un-repeatable, is for the purpose of rescuing the whole human family. But since that gift of salvation has to be perceived and welcomed and experienced by people, there certainly has been variation in the way we describe it. These are some of the emphases we may recognize.

There is the very simple approach, 'Lord, I am in trouble. Save me', and then, 'The Lord saved me, that is salvation.' This very basic understanding is much repeated in the Psalms and has most to do with the cruel experiences of everyday life, sickness, isolation, oppression, hunger, defeat. In these dark places of every human life there is prayer to be saved, lifted up and given a fresh opportunity; perhaps the most

instinctive and universal of all prayers. The prime
model in history is the Exodus, which was celebrated in
so many of the Psalms and is the key to so much Jewish
piety, for there was the agony, the pain, the prayer and
the deliverance. It is the paradigm of salvation.

At a rather deeper level, this emphasis on deliverance
is seen as the rescue from the realm of death and entry
into the realm of light and peace. Here it is the eternal
struggle which is the setting for salvation through
Christ, that infinite war between good and evil, focussed
in cross and resurrection. We all become protagonists,
and the grip of evil is strong. Only the strong Son of
God can release us by his own entry into the very heart
of the battle, by his wounds and by his ultimate victory.
This would seem to be the main emphasis in I Peter 1.
9–10 where the apostle, very conscious of present
struggles, has confidence in this deliverance which is
called 'the salvation of your souls'. Although we may
not be saved from the pains or sorrows of human life,
yet salvation is a sure gift because it has brought us into
the very presence of the Father.

As somewhat of a sideline there was a further development in mediaeval thought, that the release has to do
with the final liberation of the human soul from purgatory to enjoy the full blessings of divine light. On a visit
to Hungary a few years ago, I was able to see the library
at Debrecen seminary where there were on display
actual certificates of indulgences as sold at the time of
Luther. It is illuminating to hold such a piece of parch-
ment with the name of the purchaser scribbled in the
corner, a physical contact with concepts of God's eternal
gift which have now largely disappeared into the mists.
There is, however, a lingering persuasion in many
Catholic traditions which stresses the great power of
Christ 'in the heavenlies', beyond the world of sense,
on the eternal ladder of the saints.

At the other side of the theological spectrum, the evangelical emphasis in theology has tended to see salvation in that immediate personal turning to Christ in faith which is termed conversion. It stresses the reality of a 'new birth' as described in John 3, and the primary requirement of faith as affirmed by Paul. Christ is to be proclaimed and those who both hear and believe, repenting of their sin and praying for forgiveness, receive that gift, are restored to communion with God and are saved. Thus many Christians remember a particular date when salvation came to them. They have confidence that, the gift having been once received, there is assurance for ever. Oliver Cromwell, on his deathbed, asked his chaplain, 'Tell me, is it possible to fall from grace?' 'No, it is not possible,' said the minister. 'Then', said the dying Lord Protector, 'I am safe, for I know that I was once in grace.' There are, perhaps, not so many ministers today who would respond with such ready conviction, but the essence of the matter is there – God's action is not to be reversed.

A further emphasis here is the conviction that salvation is God's answer to the universal reality of sin, which constantly bedevils even the best human efforts and the wisest human minds and the most loving human hearts. The punishment for sin which I deserve (for repudiating God's way of life) would be darkness and death, but God's gift is freedom from the burden of guilt and that new beginning which is at the heart of forgiveness. The traditional teaching about original sin was a way of describing the tendency in us all to corrupt the good things which God has provided for us, and from which we are not rescued by the legal or habitual framework of life. It is this release from the burden of guilt, as in Bunyan's *Pilgrim's Progress*, which sets us on our road as free men and women; the action of God to set us free is focussed in the acceptance by Jesus Christ of the punishment which was wholly undeserved. The bill was paid. The cross is our salvation.

A distinctive emphasis has been the ingrafting of individuals into the body of Christ, the church. Salvation can be seen as the context in which the church lives; it is the saved community, the assembly of those who have repudiated the way of the world and accepted the way of Christ. If this is so, then it may be claimed that 'outside the church there is no salvation' and that baptism, as the rite of initiation into the church, is the mark of God's salvation offered to each person. Such a view stresses the corporate character of faith. We are never isolated souls, but we enter into faith through the teachings of the church and we are held to Christ by the ordinances of the church. We can link this with the gift of the Spirit which was given to the disciples as a group at Pentecost and which filled them with that sense of 'common life' which John calls *koinonia*, a sharing of experience and meaning with God and with the church (I John 1.3, 7).

Another very distinct view of salvation is to link it with the coming of the kingdom of God in the very presence and ministry of Jesus Christ. 'Today this scripture has been fulfilled in your hearing,' Jesus told the synagogue crowd at Nazareth when he had read the great vision of Isaiah. In a rather different style Mark also records the start of the ministry with similar words, 'The time is fulfilled and the kingdom of God is at hand; repent and believe the gospel' (Mark 1.15). Thus all the longing for the reign of God, his peace and justice and healing, became present and visible in the ministry of Christ, for there the poor were lifted up, the blind given sight and the mourners given joy and the chains of fear were smashed. So salvation comes into the world wherever this ministry is renewed; it is not a distant dream but a present reality. The resurrection means that the ministry of Jesus is not finished but continues in his body, the church, which is called to live out the kingdom peace in its own life and so reveal the eternal salvation in the present life of the world.

I have sketched these views very briefly and incompletely, not to pretend any catalogue of theological positions but to illustrate the fact that the understanding of salvation changes with the centuries and with the context. There is only one coming of the eternal word into the world as a man, one cross, one empty tomb, one God who reaches out to the world for rescue and completeness and the fruit of the creation. But our reception of God's gift is conditioned by our cast of mind, training, devotional life and often by family tradition. We look towards God's saving grace through spectacles which are bifocal, both individual and social. The lens is individual since each person has a unique history and individuality. It is social because we are all affected by the great movements of our day. Here I note some of these movements which, I believe, are shaping our current understanding of salvation.

Most widespread and relentless is the dissolution of our perception of a world of the spirit, a process which has continued for at least two centuries, largely undramatic, often meeting pockets of Christian resistance, but touching us all. By dissolution I mean that in this period the people of the western world have gradually lost an awareness of another dimension of being, a world out there, up there, beyond all knowledge but constantly impinging on our daily life. This older awareness was part of the human context of the incarnation. The Bible is a record of a people who had no difficulty at all in conversing with angels. They could hear the voices of the divine world. Similar claims could be made for the other great faith areas of the world, for it was one of the most widespread of human assumptions that the spirits who lived beyond our sight were fully involved in our affairs. The witch, the witch-doctor, the guru, the shaman, the oracle were all testimony to this constant opening of windows between the other world and this.

But slowly, over many years, we have become less and less sure of that other world and of its involvement with ours. Perhaps the hierarchy of angels was the first to go. Cherubs and seraphs, angels and archangels, who were very real to generations of believers, seem to us more like the beautiful design of heavenly wallpaper, a poetic backcloth, than living beings. It is still lovely but no longer real. Throughout these last two centuries there has been sporadic resistance. The poet Francis Thompson could write

> The angels keep their ancient places;
> Turn but a stone, and start a wing!
> 'Tis ye, 'tis your estranged faces
> That miss the many-splendoured thing.

But even he had to use antique language to make his verse. The poets have been great defenders of the spiritual realm – Masefield, Chesterton, Betjeman – in a stream of thought that attempted to turn a tide, but all have about them a nostalgia for an age that has departed. Similarly, in the more specifically Christian theology area the Oxford Movement was a nineteenth-century expression of the resistance. Newman, Keble, Froude and Ward lived in a piety which made the spiritual eternities a matter of daily conversation, to be witnessed in every church ceremony, to be guarded in every ministry. Much of their effort was unproductive, filtering through the Church of England to become argument about candles and vestments, but in essence they were rebelling against a pragmatism in the church and for a reflection on earth of the realm above.

Despite such defenders, the new context affects us all. It is much harder for us to talk about eternal life, and to know what we are talking about, than it was for the great Reformation preachers. Declarations about salvation which focus on the pains of hell – as in much of the preaching of Whitefield and Wesley – just do not carry the same force for a generation which assumes that death is simply the full stop. This means that we all tend to view salvation much more in terms of this life than the next. The gospel itself is at risk if we allow this influence to dominate us altogether, for then we would cease to believe in the transcendent God and the wonder of the incarnation, but it would be foolish to deny that our vision has become more earth-centred through the whole process of secularism. It is the over-ready acceptance of the secular world view that has led some theologians, Don Cupitt for example, to reject the validity of that spiritual realm as a primary basis of faith. For many of us it is not rejection or denial that is necessary, but rather a humble agnosticism regarding the world beyond our sight. We want to experience salvation now; God is in the present tense; we can leave the future to him since the nature and purpose we see in Christ is the for-ever-and-ever of God. I believe that this does not, and must not, amount to a denial of spiritual life which is eternal, but that we can confess much ignorance with a good conscience.

A second major influence on most Christians, certainly those in Britain, is the evident pluralism which is here to stay. For people who have always lived as a small Christian minority among powerful religious systems, this has always been the experience, but for the old Christian heartlands, where most of the church's theology has been written, it is new. It is a very considerable social change, demanding much patient work on all sides. It is also a theological frontier. In traditional theology we have been accustomed to a view of salvation that this is exclusively a way for Christian believers, that all others are in blind alleys and that the Christian gift is to be offered to all, with massive conversion to Christ as the great hope. Such a view is much easier to sustain within a strong Christian society (such as Italy in the counter-Reformation period, or as Britain in the early nineteenth century) than in places on the fringe of the Christian world.

Once again, it would be quite foolish to allow this new experience to swamp our traditional understanding. The commission to teach and baptize the nations was itself a moment of extraordinary boldness in the face of an uncomprehending world. The meaning of the incarnation is not to be drained away just because we find a mosque next door. One of the weaker responses among Christians is to accept, in innocence but also in self-doubt, that all religions are much the same and therefore the call to conversion no longer applies. We cannot sustain such a position and still speak of an apostolic faith. Yet something has happened to us in the experience; we are in a learning process. First, we are being taught to look honestly at the faith of others. For too long Christians have parodied other faiths by headlining their worst aspects or examples, while carefully concealing the grim features of Christianity through the ages. We know that the only proper relationship is to place the best beside the best, and to acknowledge that in every faith the best is not our everyday portrait. When we do this we learn respect, and that is the ground for every fruitful inter-faith meeting. Second, we are learning that the greater our trust in God the less we can exclude his blessing upon others. We cannot truly worship the God and Father of us all while maintaining that he has confined his truth and light and holiness and tears and peace to Christians alone. We might be small-minded, but God never. So we begin to expect signs of God's gifts in the insights and experience of other faiths. But there is a third strand to our learning that is more uncomfortable. When we study the history of Christian missionary expansion we soon discover that rapid, sometimes spectacular, growth has occurred when Christians have approached primitive or primal religion, tribal deities, local shrines, unwritten sagas and all that is contained under the heading of animism, but that very small progress has been made in the last two centuries when the mission has been directed towards the trained, literate, committed followers of the major faiths. This may, of course, be due to the inadequate character of our witness, to insufficient love or failure in our language. But it may also be due to the equivalence (not equality) of spiritual systems which have their own inner logic and their own outward disciplines.

This is a powerful influence on us as we attempt to say what salvation means. We will tend more and more to affirm the grace brought home to us in Christ but not to deny the possibility that others too have been offered God's light in their life of faith. We will preach Christ crucified, still a stumbling block and offence to so many, believing that there we see God plain and know that he is always our healer, but we will preach with humility because our Lord chose that road. That links with a further major influence on our thinking about salvation. It is the map of misery. Although we did not spot it at the time, a crucial step in human awareness came that day during the Vietnam war when television in the United States and in Europe brought us pictures of a terrified little girl running naked down the road after being caught by burning napalm, crying for help. The full effect of political decisions was brought into our living rooms and it sickened us. From then on we have lived with the guilty conscience of those who rest in an island of affluence in that map of human misery. So we become aware that Christian theology has all too often been taught and written by those protected by the fabric of strong churches and wealthy nations and endowed colleges. We now have to listen to the expressions of faith that come from the other side of the river, from the oppressed, the hungry, the defeated and the handicapped who trust in God's salvation, and who need it now before they die. Present action and ultimate hope run together. Bread and living bread are not far apart. For millions of our fellow citizens in the global village a sermon on immortality would have the accent of an insult, and the matchstick arms reaching out for food need more than a wafer.

All these influences shape our understanding. We may protest that the contemporary scene should not touch so central a matter as the meaning of salvation. We can hear that protest. Why do you allow what is temporary, a mere swing in the tale of human philosophies, to affect the sublime teaching of the apostles? The answer is plain. We have no option. To profess that there are no changes in our understanding would be to deny our mortality and to pretend that we are untouched by the world we inhabit and help to fashion. Even those who most stoutly defend a classical theology (by which is usually meant a western European theology), are themselves shaped in their defensive posture by the habits of thought, the assailing voices and the alarming images of the day. One of the most significant signs of this comes from eastern Europe, where the Orthodox churches are fully devoted to the peace campaigns which figure so large in the communist party agenda. The churches have been supporting peace movements with argument, prayer and preaching. We may applaud when we think how little most of our own churches are doing in this matter. But the fact of this Orthodox involvement is itself a shift of emphasis away from the peace of God, to be known only in the heavenly city, which is God's gift alone, and which was held by Augustine to be the great blessing of the divine community (*City of God* XV: xi). It may not be a shift in doctrine, but surely a shift in perception as to where the priorities lie, and thus a new view on the work of Christ.

I do not find this alarming, but it can become so if we neglect the for-ever character of the saving gift itself. The central, unchanging reality is that God draws people, through faith in Christ, into life with him. That life is only possible through forgiveness and acceptance; it is made plain in Jesus; it is established in the Holy Spirit; it is not conditional on the span of years we survive in our physical life, but unless it affects that life it is not yet real at all. Further, it becomes sustainable and visible as we enter the common life of the people of God. Our descriptions of 'life-with-God' will always vary, but the intention of God towards us does not. The action we call salvation is that movement of God towards us which sets us free from our disobedient or disbelieving life to be at one with him. It is a dealing with sin through the very character of the cross, the total offering of love, always declaring the heart of God.

In recent years we have heard another view put forward by Raymond Fung, of the World Council of

Churches, who has written about salvation as not only rescue from sin but also from being sinned-against. For those millions of people who, in daily experience, know the cruelty of poverty, the undiminished power of oppressors or the fear of unscrupulous employers there are sins to be dealt with, but they are the sins of those who do evil towards the more defenceless part of the human family. If salvation is to be made plain in the world, then there must be hope and rescue there.

I believe that a contemporary understanding of salvation will include this element but that it cannot be pushed too far. It needs to be there. We cannot, in our generation, close our eyes to what causes great suffering and pain, nor can we divorce the 'life abundant' in Christ from this present existence. To do so would be to return to an other-worldly faith which permits and thus encourages injustice. Yet if we press this too far we reach positions of impossibility. For we can all claim to be 'sinned-against'. The war widow still suffers the loss of a partner, the public figure is demeaned by newspaper gossip, the business manager is intrigued against by ambitious colleagues, the housewife is burdened with a gambling husband, and even the stolid commuter is harrassed by cattle-truck treatment on the London underground. We can all make a case. 'They' have done it to me. And we know of no release from all of this through the coming of God in Christ. The military jackboot was not removed from Palestine, nor the heaviest persecution from the infant Christian community. Indeed, Jesus spoke of even worse things in store in days ahead. If they do this killing when the wood is green and the sap of spiritual life is rising, what will they do when the wood is old and dry and the arson mentality grows? Run for the hills? But there will be no security there, and even as they flee people will be snatched away. It was a very grim scenario. Jesus stood in the line of prophetic figures who saw no easy solution but rather the cumulative effects of lives and systems directed against the way of God. We cannot doubt that the purpose of God, shown in Christ, is to remove all these disabilities and cruelties from human life. The fullness of salvation must include that vision. But there is a present tense. Even while the oppression continues, the mercy of God is active and people are drawn into a lively faith which gives them fresh hope and fresh energy to encompass even oppressors with the forgiving spirit of Christ. We have seen it happen. The fact of salvation cannot depend on the removal of all the agonies inflicted by nature and human evil, but neither, I believe, is it completed until that far wider healing of society is revealed. Salvation as an individual welcome by God into his peace and joy cannot be the end of the process, leaving millions in ignorance and sorrow. It is the essential step which begins our pilgrimage, it is a decisive turning in a new direction and a release from the burdens of our past history, but there is more to God's saving purpose, more wisdom of the cross to be known, more powers of darkness to be resisted, more children to be given proper food, more chains to be broken and more minds to be nourished in the lively word.

4

The Language of Faith

There is no point in worship which carries greater assurance of continuity than the saying of the creed. At this point the congregation is joined to the mediaeval saints, to princes of the church, to patriarchs and metropolitans, to Russian peasants and Jesuit missionaries, to the fishermen of Polynesia and the knights of Malta, to the popes and the penitents of the ages. So it seems, and so we are strengthened in the corporate life of the church. Indeed, the credal formula has provided one of the basic forms of unity, unity in the one faith. It was significant that when the World Council of Churches began its lengthy work on Confessing the Apostolic Faith, there was no other commonly accepted basis than the Nicene Creed. But it is also significant that some Christian churches very rarely use the ancient creeds in worship, some avoiding such formulae altogether and some choosing to write their own contemporary statements.

There are several reasons for such abstention. There are many Christians who use no written liturgical material for regular worship, and among them the Religious Society of Friends stands out as having consciously rejected anything which would confine the faith by defining it. Others honour the creeds but rarely use them in worship, believing that the scripture readings and the hymns are a more adequate way of expressing faith. There has been a widespread fear among non-conformists that once a creed is widely used and accepted it becomes a test which everyone has to pass, and thus a human measure of God's immeasurable grace. Having myself been brought up in that tradition it is only slowly that I have come to study the creeds more carefully and to acknowledge how important they have been in both mission and unity. In mission they have provided the most compressed teaching implement among young Christians across the variety of cultures. In 1919 the Congregational and Presbyterian churches in China had developed to the point of union discussions. That union was based on the 'acknowledgment of the Apostles' Creed as expressing the fundamental doctrines of our common evangelical faith'. The historian adds that 'mention of the Apostles' Creed was due to the strong action of the Chinese pastors. The British missionaries would have left the matter more vague, but this did not at all meet the minds of the Chinese pastors.'[1] From the days of the Jesuit missions to Latin America and Francis Xavier in India, the same story could be told of the need for unambiguous statements of the doctrines of the faith which can be learnt even when they cannot be fully understood. So there is in the creed an element of test which we need, a test of the full or comprehensive character of our proclamation of the gospel. Those who 'would have left the matter more vague' ran the risk of highly individualized bias in the teachers of the faith, and increasing vagueness in each generation of believers.

As well as being a tool for effective mission, the creeds may yet be a sign of unity. This is certainly the hope of Anglicans, who included the creeds in the Lambeth Quadrilateral as a foundation stone on which

[1] Norman Goodall, *History of the London Missionary Society*, OUP 1954, p. 218.

the true church is built. As we are linked in faith across the centuries, so we have confidence that we are not solitary believers, persuaded only by personal experience. The creeds thus stand alongside the great prayers of Islam, which also present a single faith expression across a multitude of cultures. Yet I have to question whether the creeds themselves present so solid and unchanging and unchallenged statements of Christian faith as we may often suppose.

All credal statements, in every age and every part of the church, are expressions of the human mind reflecting on the mystery of God. So they are limited. The limitation is one of human expression, for a few words never do justice to all that is revealed in Christ. The words only sketch the barest outline. The words also were written at one point of history and so have their contemporary meanings which are inevitably amended in translation. Further, the creeds have usually been the response of the church to particular challenges, and so they stress a particular doctrine which was a prime necessity at that time. The emphasis may not be necessary now, and statements much needed now may not be there.

If we look at the Apostles' Creed, these limitations become plain. Although it was first commonly used in the sixth century its basis goes back much earlier, certainly to the latter part of the second century. At that period one of the toughest arguments among Christians was to do with the teaching of Marcion. He believed in a dual system of good and evil powers, with the evil power being responsible for the human nature and body which tends to evil. He saw a sharp distinction between old and new testaments, believing that the God of the Old Testament has nothing to do with the grace we see in Jesus Christ; law and grace were in

opposition. Jesus had come to reveal, with total reliability, the God of love, unknown before, and had taken
the appearance of a human being. He regarded the
writings of Paul as the most authoritative manual of
theology and the Gospel of Luke as the most reliable
account of Jesus. Against all this the church needed to
build defences. Trusting in one God who is the sole
creator, there could be no room for two equal powers,
and if that creator is good and holy there could be no
write-off of the human personality as the work of the
evil one. To speak of Jesus having the appearance of a
man was to undermine the basis of incarnation, that he
became a man. So in this early creed we note specific
stress on

the creator of heaven and earth;
he suffered, was crucified, died and was buried;
he descended to the dead (or 'to hell');
the resurrection of the body.

By linking heaven and earth together in this way the
church was proclaiming no ultimate separation into the
realms of good and evil; all are the work of one God,
however much the world may be marred by the extraordinary aptitude of human beings to corrupt all parts
of the creation. This statement affirmed the Old
Testament which was uncompromising about the one
all-encompassing Creator.

The actual physical suffering of Jesus was stressed. It
was no mere shadow. He was physically nailed to the
wood and there he died. The church could not live by a
seeming Christ, a shadow figure ultimately untouched
by human crises.

The phrase about the descent into hell is, to us, a very
strange one and few of us can say this creed with much
awareness of its meaning. It is frequently interpreted to

say that there is no zone so evil, no night so black that it is out of bounds to the Son of God. While that is a splendid message, I doubt whether it was the original intention which was probably closer to a missionary journey to the spirits of the dead, caught in endless, wandering sorrow, or even a journey consigned to that same fate. The repeated use in Acts of the phrase 'from the dead' (rather than 'from death') suggests this. Is it necessary to believe this? I am not persuaded that it is. To believe in the universal saving power of God in Christ is one thing; to believe in the Friday to Sunday journey of Christ in spirit to the realm of the dead is quite another, which I have to leave in the area of faithful supposition.

We are in much the same position regarding the 'resurrection of the body'. It conjures up for us a Stanley Spencer vision of the graveyard with the tombs beginning to creak open and the reconstituted hands groping upwards and the bodies levering awkwardly to their feet, a grotesque Gothic film. Two major strands of thought lie behind the phrase. The first was the rejection of Marcion's dualism, to assent that the body is not so essentially evil that it cannot be saved, and by the body we need to understand the whole human personality which cannot be envisaged without a body. The whole 'me' is what God is concerned about. Nothing is left to the authority of evil. Second, the New Testament points unarguably to climactic events which are not far off. The apostles expected that as they were witnesses to the resurrected and ascended Christ, so they would be witnesses to the triumphant Christ, and it was only slowly that they realized a longer time span would be involved. So resurrection was frequently described in terms of that great final round of the struggle when 'we shall all be changed in a flash, in the

twinkling of an eye, at the last trumpet-call' (I Cor.15.52).
For us today that kind of celestial gathering is hard to
talk about with any assurance, for the time span is now
beyond our vision. So it is more general today for us to
spiritualize the whole concept and see it as a reference
to our continuing personalities in a wholly non-bodily
form, a thesis based not on logic but on faith. So we
grapple feebly with knowledge of a spiritual world
now over-ridden by the material and physical which
dominate our lives.

In the Apostles' Creed, therefore, we recognize both a
local, contemporary bias at source and a shift in understanding through the years. The same is true for the
Nicene Creed. At that point in Christian history when
the General Council of the church met at Nicea, the
great issues at debate concerned the trinitarian understanding of God and the incarnation in Jesus. The major
dissident was Arius, the great orthodox theologian
Athenasius, and the magisterial chairman the emperor
Constantine. The question was being pressed whether
Jesus was the Son of God through birth or through a gift
which came at his baptism, whether he was subordinate
to God the Father, and whether in his life he was
himself a dualism with a divine nature alongside a
human nature. Similarly, is the Holy Spirit truly God; is
the Spirit sent or directed by God the Father, and did
the Spirit first come to humanity at Pentecost? In the
midst of such debate, often violent, the statement of
belief was formed to represent the majority view. It
is designed to deal with these specific issues. The
Christian thinkers of the fourth century had to use
the concepts and language at hand, and found that
pre-Christian Greek words were the best they had to
describe the mystery of the Trinity, and these were
translated into Latin with some variation of meaning. So

we get 'of one Being with the Father' or 'of one sub-
stance with the Father', and the repeated affirmation
'God from God, Light from Light, true God from true
God'. Jesus is 'begotten, not made', thus distinguishing
Jesus from the creation. He 'came down from heaven',
for the three-decker universe was then still the most
popular concept, and 'was made man'. What is stressed
is the eternal Christ, fully and gloriously God, who
visited us in his humanity to suffer precisely human
affliction and death, and then returned through resurrection and ascension to be with the eternal Father
of all. This parabola is fully sustained by the New
Testament, particularly in the writings of Paul and John,
and is the view we call orthodox. Arius was defeated,
and his view 'that the Son has a beginning but that God
is without beginning' was then labelled heretical, although controversy continued for many years.

   The christology which we inherit in this way is very
difficult to expound in modern words, and I suspect
that most of us simply decline to teach it in any detail.
Many conundrums are posed for the modern mind.
What could be the relation of the eternal life of the
Trinity to that span of thirty years when Christ was on
earth? Thirty years has a span in history, but can be only
part of the 'now' for eternity. So can we say that the
trinitarian God was bereft of the Son for a span? And
was Jesus in his flesh separated from the Father (so that
he could pray to the Father as we do), or still as closely
bound to the divine life as in eternity (so that those who
see Christ see the Father)? We have to confess to the
great mystery of the incarnation, which our minds
cannot fully grasp, to which the scriptures witness, and
which the Council at Nicea did not explain. When
Christians today recite the Nicene Creed they testify to
the potent arguments of Arius which had to be defeated

sixteen hundred years ago, but which are not our primary concern as we seek to be disciples of Christ.

It is only fair to look also at a modern creed to note the bias today. I take, because I am familiar with it, the Confession of Faith of the United Reformed Church, prepared in 1972. It is interesting to note that its language is already dated, and I have provided alternate readings where the church has become dissatisfied with sexist terminology.

We believe in one living and true God,
creator, preserver and ruler of all things in heaven
    and earth,
Father, Son and Holy Spirit:
    Him alone we worship and in him we put our trust.
We believe that God, in his infinite love for the world,
    (for men) gave his eternal Son, Jesus Christ our
    Lord, who became man,
lived on earth in perfect love and obedience,
died upon the cross for our sins,
rose again from the dead;
    And lives for evermore, saviour, judge and king.
We believe that, by the Holy Spirit,
this glorious gospel is made effective
so that through faith we receive the forgiveness of
    sins,
newness of life as children of God
and strength in the present world to do his will.
We believe in one, holy, catholic and apostolic Church,
in heaven and on earth,
wherein by the same Spirit
the whole company of believers is made one Body of
    Christ:
    To worship God and serve him and all people (all
    men)

in his Kingdom of righteousness and love.
We rejoice in the gift of eternal life,
and believe that, in the fullness of time,
God will renew and gather in one all things in Christ,
to whom with the Father and the Holy Spirit
be glory and majesty, dominion and power,
both now and for ever. Amen.

What is significant for our purpose is that this confession has far less to say about the character of the
divine life than the Nicene Creed, and far more about
the life of people in relation to God. The focus has
shifted. We do not speak about the virgin birth or
the resurrection of the body. But we retain the old
adjectives which define the church and set the confession within the context of worship at the beginning
and the end. Within the United Reformed Church we
would claim that there is sufficient identity here
with the ancient creeds for there to be continuity, and
sufficient distinctness for this to be our own confession.

All credal statements reflect their origins in date and
place; they are limited expressions of what is believed;
they cannot be made absolute as if handed down on the
mountain in tablets of stone. We can say that they are
the best instrument available and therefore of permanent
value, but the greater weight placed on them the less
valuable they become. Use them as a witness to the faith
as seen at one point of Christian history, and we can all
rejoice and thank God for such clarity and range. We
can sing such a creed with devotion even when particular words may be hard for us, just as we can sing
a Wesley or Watts hymn without giving intellectual
assent to every phrase. But once we make the creeds
into a final, authoritative, comprehensive definition of
what must be believed, then the human limitations
come fully into view and many of us will remain silent.

This is the risk which is taken by all who would define doctrine in a very authoritarian way. We take human words, with all their complexity and limitations, as the definition of what is beyond words, and so impose a human boundary on the grace of God. We take the understanding of our own period and attempt to impose it on all future ages. We take our thinking about the gift of God in Christ, our deductions or interpretations, and place them before the gift itself. It is for these reasons that I regard the proclamation of Papal Infallibility in 1870 as one of the most serious errors that Christians have made in doctrinal matters, one that is very difficult to reverse and which presents a great barrier to any approach to the fullness of unity. It was an action which placed the statements of a pope, when made on matters of faith and morals and when made as universal pontiff, above the limitations of human statements and so made them universally applicable. The words used in 1870 are significant:

> It is a dogma divinely revealed that the Roman Pontiff, when he speaks ex-cathedra, that is, when in the discharge of the office of pastor and doctor of all Christians, by virtue of his supreme apostolic authority he defines a doctrine regarding faith and morals to be held by the universal Church, by the divine assistance promised to him in blessed Peter, is possessed of that infallibility with which the divine Redeemer willed that his Church should be endowed for defining doctrine regarding faith and morals; and that therefore such definitions of the Roman Pontiff are irreformable of themselves, and not from the consent of the Church (*Pastor Aeternus*).

This was an extraordinary leap in the declared powers of a human priest, however much may have been assumed for the preceding centuries. The church always longs for infallibility. To be able to proclaim doctrine which is guaranteed absolutely right for all people in every century, with no alteration possible ever, that is the dream of all authoritarian religions. It brings divine knowledge, the very sight of God, on to a piece of paper dated this month and this year and signed by a pope. Having once declared that, how do you ever escape from it, for the 1870 decree must itself be infallible?

Yet when it was implemented in 1950 to declare the doctrine of the bodily assumption of the Virgin Mary (a second phase to the declaration in 1854 of the immaculate conception) the Roman Catholic church was committed to a belief which had no historical basis. No apostolic writer knew of it. Such belief was certainly very general in the Catholic church since the Middle Ages, when devotion to Mary had become the most popular of all prayers. But to add these elements to the core of Christian doctrine was a very significant step which failed to distinguish between the gospel of salvation and popular devotion. The pope was infallible but he was wrong.

Protestantism, however, does not find it easy either. Here the longing for eternally valid statements looks to the verbal inerrancy of the Bible or to highly acclaimed individual interpreters. Naturally these are not all agreed and so we find a diversity of teaching, for example, on predestination to salvation. We thus have every reason to acknowledge the conditional quality of all statements of doctrine. Many human factors enter into their wording, not only the cultural and contemporary elements but personal history too, the way a group has been led through the years and how loyalty to the truth is understood.

But beyond the limitations of Catholic and Protestant credal formulae there remains a blessed reality, that God's great word to the world was not a word but a life. What was incarnated cannot be wholly inverbated. The words are essential for the transmission of both facts and meanings, but they never convey all that the presence of a person does. The unchangeable factor is always that Christ has come; the doctrinal formulations which describe that event are never final, complete or inerrant.

Does this entail a morass of conflict, doubt, diversity and schism? This has been a great fear in the minds of Catholic and Orthodox Christians through the centuries. How can we present a united witness in a world of powerful religions unless we have a certain basis of doctrine, or a united influence in a world of relative values unless we can state absolutes? Is this not one of the sad realities of modern liberal thought, that the strength is sapped from the declarations of faith as they themselves are seen as conditional? I would reply, first, that the point of strength and authority and permanence has to be the divine intervention in the life of the world. We need have no hesitation in declaring that in Jesus we find word, action, attitude and will that are always directed to the glory of God, wholly reliable, to be trusted and followed. Second, we can say with confidence that the central teaching of the apostles about the nature and purpose of God revealed in Jesus is the central teaching of the church through the ages. Third, that the words in which such teaching is conveyed must vary according to the culture and the life issues of each people. Fourth, that there is a penumbra of teaching, outside the core, which does not need to be treated as permanently binding because it has arisen from one particular context in the life of the people of

God. Fifth, the distinction between the permanent and
the temporary teaching can only be made with difficulty,
in humility and subject to further light on our pilgrimage into the mystery of God. And sixth, just as all
our words are inadequate, so are our actions. We never
fully reveal Christ in our lives. So while we strive for
both orthodoxy and orthopraxis we do not claim the
fullness of either, knowing that the Lord has much still
to teach us of his unending grace.

5

Tabernacles and Temples

In London the very informal nature of a series of annual classical concerts has become transmuted into an elaborate ritual, so that on one night of the summer a great audience becomes wildly intoxicated by second-rate music, behaves as though with midsummer madness, puts a laurel wreath on a bust, and waves the national flag as though Buckingham Palace is being threatened by enemy howitzers. As for cricket... the institution has almost taken over the game, so that as much time and effort is spent on club politics as on the field. We love to make institutions. There we are comforted. We know what to do and when to do it. We know what to wear when asked to a garden party. In this way the British made comfortable the extraordinary diversities and cruelties of an empire, weaving the institutional net around the extremes of morality and habit found around the globe. So we know how this is done and how readily we fall in with it. We are not surprised that it happened to Christianity.

Was this the intention of Jesus? We find very little reference to it in his words or in the way he organized his immediate followers. The itinerant preacher seems to have expected that his followers would also be travellers, sharing a message of the reign of God with all sorts of people, facing opposition partly because they were outsiders who had no seats in the institutions of religion. We find only two references to the church in the gospels, both in Matthew (16.18 and 18.17) yet so much has been built upon them that it is like an upended pyramid balancing on a fragile point. Jesus focussed chiefly on the relation of people to God and thus to each other, on forgiveness, generosity, service, faithfulness and sacrifice, on the simplicity of children, on life's critical choices, on the treasure of God's presence. So we find no instructions about the shape and style of church organization, its methodology, its law. All this was the development of the centuries.

It was a necessary development. Wandering preachers and occasional miracles and individual interpreters are a possible basis for a short-term uprising of a faith, a sudden spurt, but could not carry forward the assured word of the gospel over a long period with both convincing argument and steady corporate worship. Christians faced persecution, so needed the support of a fellowship. New leaders needed training and authority to speak. Some way of binding together people of very different cultural background had to be discovered. All this argued for organization. So while the gospels indicate that Jesus provided no blueprint for a continuing institution we can only be thankful that one came into being, for without it we should never have heard of Jesus Christ. There are moments when we wish that tabernacles were the model for the church, tents which could be taken down, temporary resting places on a long trek, but in our hearts we know that the living of the faith in a settled society needs the reliability and presence of an institution, just as the temple succeeded the tabernacle. The great risk that is run throughout Christian history is then to invest the pragmatic institution with the same authority and permanence as the gospel itself.

During the very early years of the church's life, as the evangelical movement developed into an abiding institution, many factors were at work. There was a pressing call for unity among the scattered Christian congregations, so that the divisions of race and class and language might not disrupt the fellowship. Such unity itself required some organism, some binding-together. This was very closely linked to the need for recognized authority, for without that unity is very difficult to hold for any length of time. Authority developed in two directions. First through people, when the event had to be faced that the apostles were old and died, and some other voices had to be found. Second through writing, when the oral traditions about Jesus became a diversity of texts; some had to be selected as having authority. These were internal pressures leading to an institutional framework. There were also external pressures. The style and customs of society affected Christians. All the cults of the Roman empire with their priests and priestesses and temples and feasts set a model for a new religious group, so that it was extremely unlikely that a young church could eschew altogether such influence in its life. As the church grew in extent, so it met the cultures of the many tribes that made up the Roman empire, each with its own chiefly structure. And the greatest influence of all was the empire itself, the primary model for the institution which was to provide a priest-king for a new world authority. All this led inevitably to a very powerful institution. Was this what Jesus intended? I think it is very unlikely that Jesus or the apostles saw anything like the shape that was to emerge in the fourth century, for organization and particularly triumphant organization was very far from their minds. The Parliamentary protesters could not see the Commonwealth, nor the first singers of the

Marseillaise the Napoleonic empire. Pioneers of great movements do not generally see their passionate commitment in terms of structures.

Yet it is precisely those first four centuries which were to provide a pattern of church life which was to become normative for hosts of Christians and sacrosanct for some. This preponderant weight given to the early centuries is partly nature and partly theology. The natural part is simply the power which the early years of an organization have in setting the outline for the future. Examples are legion. The way in which the Oxford and Cambridge colleges were founded and fashioned as Christian endowments has remained for centuries the mould for quite different educational needs, whether or not that mould is most beneficial. Barristers are still called to the bar and the Commons still march to the Lords to listen to the monarch read the Prime Minister's speech. But in the case of the church there is a theological dimension to this effect. The teaching of Jesus Christ is primary for all that was to follow, and the apostles were the closest of his companions, receiving his constant teaching and thus our surest guides to the way of the Lord. The Holy Spirit was given to them to guide them into all truth. Thus we can have confidence in the apostolic church as very close to the mind of Christ. So, it may be argued, those who followed immediately after the apostles, the Timothy generation, were in the next best position to plan the church according to Christ. The early church has this aura and holiness. Its influence on all that succeeded was therefore vast.

I believe this has been a dangerous argument, the tendency of which is to dignify one historic period with quite unnecessary permanence. If it is true that those Christians who lived three or four generations from

Christ are particularly trustworthy guides then the decreasing realiability of later generations must land us in a position of utter ignorance. Just as there is no evident increase of wisdom or spiritual insight over the centuries, so there is no evident decrease either. The early Christians could make mistakes just as we can, and those who led them sometimes led them astray. There can be no other conclusion from the history of sometimes bitter quarrels which developed over Christian thought and practice, issues arousing passion and abuse. People specially endowed with early-generation-wisdom would have avoided such clashes because they would have known the mind of Christ. This becomes the more obvious when we realize that many Christians in the early and mediaeval church were very ill-informed, isolated and dependent on occasional itinerant preachers for their knowledge of Christ. Some church authorities fastened on ignorance of the laity as the key to a successful use of power. So any image of the ancient church as an angelic bearer of light and truth which must be followed at all costs is very far from reality.

As we consider this strange institution which has carried the name of Christ across the generations and continents, which has been formed by many cultural factors and which has always attempted to write its own history, there are two issues which press me. One is the attracting and repelling power of the institution itself, and the relation of that power to the gospel. The other is the presence and meaning of the Holy Spirit in the church.

The first issue is forced on us when we ask, How does the drawing power of Christ on the cross connect with the drawing power of the church? So often the very opposite appears to be the case, for those in the Christian church who attract the largest crowds of eager listeners, especially in Europe and North America, appear as speakers who attract people to themselves. This has been true of great preachers through the ages. That splendid voice, the dignified bearing, the oratory of the Victorian preachers filled the pews. The handsome features and sizzling remarks of the TV evangelist draw the viewers. And while that happens on one level, there are those magisterial, grey, lined faces of the elderly priests that draw the faithful to mass and confession. There is the music of the cathedral choir, lilting and floating up to the carved bosses on the vaulting, as the psalm tells of divine victory. And there is the blessed quietness of the Friends Meeting House, dignified plain brick and white framed sash windows looking over a lawn with lilac trees. So many attractions. What of all that is the permanent call of the one Christ and what is the ephemera of a social institution?

The other side of the coin is the repelling quality of the church. A letter from the Taizé community asks the question, How is it that when so many church leaders are eager to help young people into faith the young generally reject the church? At a conference on the missionary challenge I heard an American speaker calling for greater effort to reach the 'untouched millions'. A quiet academic got up and said, 'It is not that they are all untouched. Millions have been touched but don't like what they see.' We recognize the reality of this because there are many features of the institutional church which make us unwilling members. There is often a small-minded criticism of people, a moral refuse collection which can make us into unpleasant gossips. Or a bigoted certainty that allows no doubt or question or further exploration. Sometimes the structures take over and ambition fuels the ministry. Or the small-town loyalty of the congregation hides for ever the glory and agony of the world church. For some it may be a liturgical style that repels, the Alternative Service Book language, too casual to be proper, or the length of the sermon. There is no shortage of repelling features. But what have they to do with the great stumbling-block of the cross of Christ?

It becomes clear that the church both attracts and repels for a host of reasons which have nothing to do with the everlasting realities of the gospel. If this is so, then any facile equation of entry into the church and eternal salvation is very questionable. Drawn to the church is not the same as drawn to Christ, and it is the latter which is the route to the cross and resurrection. This distinction is all the more necessary if we have a high view of the church, thinking of it as the body of Christ or as the extension of the incarnation. 'Outside the church there is no salvation' is only tenable if we are free to define church as the total community of Christian believers, and not as any one visible part of that community. Similarly we can thank God for so many who are drawn to Christ, who seek his way in their lives, and who trust his living presence, for whom the institution does not seem to be the essential hand-maid of belief. I find it hard to understand these people fully, but acknowledge their sincerity and wish we could see their gifts infusing the institutional life. We need to see the church more as a servant of the gospel than as the gospel itself. Life in the church is not heaven. Christ is head of the body, but the body is sometimes disobedient, often wounded, often dirty. While we open the word of God and preach it, we must not presume to be it.

What then do we mean when we confess belief in the one, holy, catholic and apostolic church? The institution we see is not one but divided, not very holy but stained, not yet catholic as embracing all, and frequently less than apostolic in its missionary obedience. One way of dealing with this is indicated in the Documents of Vatican II.

Christ, the one Mediator, established and cease-lessly sustains here on earth His holy Church, the community of faith, hope and charity, as a visible structure. Through her He communicates truth and grace to all. But the society furnished with hierar-chical agencies and the Mystical Body of Christ are not to be considered as two realities, nor are the visible assembly and the spiritual community, nor the earthly Church and the Church enriched with hea-venly things. Rather they form one interlocked reality which is comprised of a divine and human element ... Just as the assumed nature inseparably united to the divine Word serves Him as a living instrument of salvation, so, in a similar way, does the communal structure of the Church serve Christ's Spirit, who vivifies it by way of building up the body (*Lumen Gentium* 1.8).

Here the two realities, heavenly and earthly, holy and sinful, are seen as dimensions of the one visible institution. This is a comforting line of development, for it provides assurance that even though the people who make up the church err in many ways yet the church as a whole retains its marks of Christ. I wonder, however, if this adequately represents human experience. I be-lieve in the one, holy, catholic and apostolic church because that is the calling of God in Christ, and that is what the Holy Spirit will create if God's people will be obedient, but it is not the institutional framework which I see and serve today. We are *in via*. During this journey there are many aspects of the church's life which do not yet reflect the person of Christ and many attractions which are as earthly as our appetites; so that the church serves best when it leads the mind and heart away from itself and simply offers a way through our possession-obsessed society to the sacrificial love of the Lord.

But what do we mean by the Holy Spirit in the church? If women and men, following Christ, pray for the Spirit to lead them, will that Spirit not enable them to avoid error, declare truth, offer forgiveness, and build the new Jerusalem? And if this is God's gift then is not the church on a single track history, always rejoicing in the past, never contradicting it, never needing a Reformation? Is this not a sure basis for the Orthodox to point to the full competence of tradition to hold the treasure of the gospel?

I believe that these serious questions have to be faced by those in the Reformed tradition, who sometimes have acted as though there is no sacred history and every generation writes on a clean page. We all have to recognize the amazing gifts of insight, obedience and love that have been shown through the ages by hosts of Christians, so the work they have done is never to be ignored. Yet the promise of Christ is that the Holy Spirit will lead or guide us into all truth (John 16.13), not that we shall arrive there without a journey. It is a very general desire and perhaps a psychological pressure for us to omit the journey and expect the Holy Spirit to bring the fullness of truth immediately through her chosen channels. To have a body of truth, a book of dogma, a constitution with rules, a complete moral code all signed, so to say, by the Holy Spirit and affirmed by the church authorities – what a relief to the searching soul. There we would have a permanent rock base for the foundation of the church.

If we have confidence in the Holy Spirit, why should we not expect this assurance? Because the Spirit illumines, teaches, leads through people just like ourselves and not in a vacuum. We have no evidence that at one period of history or in one part of the world or at one level of church life men and women were wholly receptive to the Holy Spirit. Always we have been looking at puzzling reflections in a mirror, or at images seen through a mist. This is not to deny the presence of the Spirit. If there is anything of eternal value and insight in the proclamation of the church, it does not arise from the vast wisdom of Christians. We do receive gifts. But we receive them very partially, within the mental framework of our culture. Our doctrine of the Holy Spirit therefore must have room for both the recognition of the Spirit's presence in the church and the limited reception of the Spirit, which allows for change and development. Continuity is assured by the fact of one historical foundation in the life of Christ, and one Spirit who leads us. Development is required because we never have an unmediated perception of the mystery of God. So the institutional church has never finally reached the union of the spiritual with the visible; it is always in process, always trusting that the Spirit will lead faithful people into truth. Our joy and confidence is that, through the gift of the Spirit, the church in every age is given sufficient knowledge of God to bring men and women into a living relation with him. What is eternal is that gift, for it is the gift of God's being; what is not eternal is the institutional framework within which the gift is perceived.

It is at that point that I find myself unable to walk together with the Vatican II statement. For while it is surely true that there is a mingling of the earthly and the spiritual, the human and the divine, in the church of God, I do not believe that these are 'interlocked' in a manner which is parallel to the incarnation. In Jesus Christ the unity of human and divine was total, so that the visible life of the man was the revealing of the very heart of God. But the church is a company of sinners. At many points in its history it has revealed not the heart of God but the wandering passions of its leaders. It is an institution subject to all the institutional pressures – to centralize authority, to create a closed inner cabinet, to demand obedience, to expect generous giving, to oppose radical thinking, to establish a legal basis – which are part of human societies. The wonder and the miracle are that even in so earthy an institution the light of the gospel breaks through. The gates of hell, which may be not just evil regimes opposing the church but also the powers of pride, ambition, egotism within the church, these cannot wholly quench the light.

I love the church. She is, in a very deep sense, my mother. I, like many thousands, have found in her a breadth of understanding and caring, a mutual support in times of trial, a reminder of the greatest gifts of God and a necessary challenge to conscience. But the more we claim for the institution, the less our claims carry conviction. Give sacred names to our ordinary business and soon the unreality shows. Speak only of sacrifice when we are dealing with power and the cynic will rightly expose us. Claim to be the kingdom of God when all the less public sins in the book are still known among us, and we diminish the vision of the gospel. The institution exists to serve the gospel, to let the gospel loose in the world and so to point away from itself to the one who calls it into being. We believe in the church, not because she is righteous but because God provides this place in human history where his call will be expressed; and not because she is the saviour but because through all the church's ambivalent history the Lord of grace has never left her alone.

6

How Institutions Change

When we are young it appears as though institutions like the church are unable to change. One definition of an institution is a body which exists long after its original purpose has disappeared. That is the voice of the cynical observer and the radical spirit, and there can be few of us who have not felt like that at some point in our lives. The processes of change are daunting. How do you shift a college of cardinals or the General Assembly of the Church of Scotland, or the house of clergy in the Synod of the Church of England? Can God shift them? All the forces are on the side of conservatism – the canon law, the civil law, the financial security, the professional attitude, the love of the institution by its best members, the long history, the very portraits of the fathers. There are few people, and none of any wisdom, who would have the church rush into radical change without care and deep consideration, but there are many who wonder whether conservatism has been too powerful an element in a body which is always ready to rest on its hassocks. All too often the church has moved too little and too late. In England the resistance to movement led the Church of England into a stand-off with the industrial revolution and the vast social change which accompanied it, a loss of empathy still affecting our religious scene.

Yet change happens. Even in the ancient and authoritarian there are changes. It takes a specialist to do justice to the movements in Catholicism in the last generation. I can testify to aspects of change in two areas of my experience – the Protestant missionary society and the achievement of a measure of church unity. They show response to two of the great stimuli of change, the first to the new facts displayed in history, the second to the logic of our belief.

For one hundred and fifty years the London Missionary Society was one of the great independent institutions, founded and run by people of conviction and enthusiasm, for sending the Gospel from Britain across the world. Its foundation followed hard on the work of William Carey and its first endeavours, at the end of the eighteenth century, were partly inspired by the voyages of Captain Cook. Its aim was to avoid any ecclesiastical base and to proclaim the Gospel without prescribing any form of church order. It is not surprising, therefore, that its finest work was in the pioneering activity of mission when individuality counted most. In the South Pacific islands, in South Africa, in Malaya and China and Hong Kong, even in Siberia, in Guyana up the Demerara river, there the LMS pioneers were called to hard service. The follow-up was not easily achieved. In England the LMS soon ceased to appeal to people in all the churches, since denominational societies were springing up and expecting loyalty, so it was largely left to the independents or Congregationalists to support the LMS. This they very effectively did for over a century. In the places where the work flourished and churches were formed there was intense discussion about the form of church life, but generally it was a reflection of what the missionaries had known at home, with themselves as the ministers in charge. Much depended on the individual and no doubt some petty popes flourished for a time. But by the grace of God many lively communities of faith were born and sustained, often in the most unpromising circumstances. It was this Society that I joined as a young Christian and through which I served as an ordained minister of the Congregational church in the islands of the South Pacific.

It is now possible to see that period of service (the 1950s and 1960s) as the concluding phase of one style of missionary activity. The minister I followed in one group of islands had worked with, and had largely been responsible for, a church constitution which described the way the Assembly and the island councils would work, but ended with the clause, 'Notwithstanding any part of this constitution it is accepted that the word of the missionary appointed by the LMS is supreme.' The man could never forget his service as an army chaplain when he reached the dizzy heights of Lieutenant Colonel; he believed that the same kind of authority produced the best results in church life. Within ten years of his retirement the colonial government was gone, an independent state had been declared and local people (with a lack of training for which we were mainly responsible) occupied the senior offices of the church and the micro-state. The same sort of thing, though I hope with less dramatic contrasts, was happening around the world. The churches, though valuing the old missionary associations, saw no basis for expatriate authority any longer. On the other side, British Christians saw little basis either. Any suggestion that the British churches had a peculiar calling to be the teachers of the world was long vanished in the general decline of western church-going. The Second World War had destroyed any image of a Christian continent. Our church base was not only smaller in numbers but uncertain in theology. Imperial confidence had fled. So a missionary society based on London began to seem anachronistic, for changes in the world had sapped its original basis for existence.

This was not a cause for tears; it was a matter for rejoicing. It was only because of the remarkable blessing of the enterprise that independent churches had come to maturity around the world. Not all the errors and eccentricities of the missionaries had held back this work of the Holy Spirit to move the hearts of men and women into faith. It was true to say that in the 1960s there was not a nation on earth without some form of Christian community, and for that we have to thank the persistent pioneers of many communions. The church in each place has the primary calling to witness to the gospel in its own society, and has at the same time to express its solidarity with the global family of Christians. That local responsibility and world-wide fellowship was not expressed in the traditional missionary society, for there key decisions taken in a London committee room by British people could affect church life in Singapore or Zambia. In such a context radical change is either resisted and resented or else welcomed, and it is not clear why one response is made rather than the other.

Within the LMS circle there was readiness for change. It came in two phases. The first was in 1966 when the independent society changed into a church related council. The primary reason for this was the request of the Congregational Church for a more structured relationship. It was increasingly felt that to have so major a sector of church life as world mission wholly outside the formal life of the denomination was a weakness which should be remedied. So the Congregational churches in the United Kingdom, Australia, and New Zealand (which were in effect the source of

LMS personnel and finance) accepted the formula of a Congregational Council for World Mission to carry forward the responsibilities of the LMS. No such change can be entirely painless (for the tug of the old way pulls at the heart), but this was relatively so. It was largely the same people doing the same kind of work but under the direction of those appointed by the churches and answerable to them.

This first small step made the next step possible. In 1975 it had become plain to most of those with responsibility in London that we were nearing the end of the one-way flow of world mission. Requests for missionary personnel were greatly reduced; in some places there were government restrictions on the entry of missionaries; in most places regional ecumenical organizations were growing in influence; in every place indigenous leadership was effective and colonial attitudes deeply resented. The only way forward was to seek new ways of relating which reflected the reality of the world church, and to do this as an international exercise. Invitations were sent to all the churches with which the LMS had been long associated, to meet in Singapore, and all accepted.

Those of us who were then on the London staff went to the meeting with a whole series of options but no very clear idea of what might emerge. In the event the main recommendation came through with surprising clarity. It was to sustain church-to-church relationships to help in the missionary enterprise, but to do so only on a basis of full mutuality and shared responsibility. In working this out over the next two years we found that the design could only be a round table at which all the churches could sit, where the major decisions would be taken, and that all the practical working out should rest upon the churches themselves rather than on the central body. We saw how easily we could slip back into missionary society attitudes. Part of the response was to recruit an international staff and there was long discussion about moving the office out of London, but the decision in the end was to stay there. In 1977 the Council for World Mission was inaugurated. It is too early to say whether the change has fulfilled all the hopes, but some gains are very evident.

The United Kingdom churches have surrendered power; they form a minority, so that even though they raise most of the contributions they do not decide the use. Further, they have themselves become applicants for help. Their need for missionaries or for grant aid is placed on the table in exactly the same way as requests from India or Samoa, and the same criteria are applied. Churches which receive personnel are expected to care for them and to pay their allowances, even though a grant from the centre is needed to meet all the bills; in this way it is the churches which employ people and are free to decide whether to continue doing so. Each church in membership is expected to contribute to the common purse and to develop knowledge of the world fellowship through its own educational programmes. A considerable programme of inter-church visits has developed, and also a method of training for mission through international groups undertaking study and projects together. Another sign that this new type of association is valuable has been applications to join from churches which had no LMS or Presbyterian tradition.

Of course there are difficulties to be faced. Two can be summarized here. One in-built problem is that as a company of churches which had a common historical link there is a confessional element which cannot be avoided. This may be seen as a competitor for attention against the ecumenical councils and agencies, a more comfortable arena where family likeness smooths the edges. Within such a company it is possible that some may participate because it is easier to be given grants of money than in ecumenical groups. So the missionary intention may be blunted as we become a rather good club. That risk has to be dealt with by exposing the Council's affairs at every point to the ecumenical critique, and possibly by dissolving the Council into a fully ecumenical round table if there are realistic plans brought forward. The other difficulty is more psychological than to do with structure. A complex operation of this sort is not easy for everyone to understand and so there can be, especially in elderly people in Britain, regret and a sense of loss because there is no direct link with overseas mission, no way of describing 'our work over there' or listening to 'our people'. This is not just paternalism and sentimentality. Mission means people, and unless we can visualize and name people then our personal commitment slackens. Since several denominations have block budgeting and transfer an annual sum to the Council, there is a loss of personal interest. So the many agencies which offer names of 'adopted' children or precisely pictured projects can win support. There is much work to be done here if we are to combine the round table with direct, bilateral involvement.

This transformation of one missionary agency is a small matter on the world scene, but is significant because it shows that when people take the history of salvation seriously then institutional change must follow. God has moved people to become disciples of Christ so that, in every land, there are churches which are to be recognized as parts of the global fellowship. In such a world the United Kingdom, European, and North American missionary societies wear the clothing of the past, portraying that calling which gave rise to the world church but which now has become an equally powerful call to drop the concepts of charity, of maturity here and immaturity there, of know-how here and ignorance there, of western power, so that all may serve equally the one cause of Christian witness.

The other institutional change I have seen at close quarters has been the inauguration of the United Reformed Church, comprising three distinctive traditions of churchmanship. Since the 1940s the work of reuniting the broken fragments of the church of God has been rising up the church agenda, as enormous world problems have been faced and as the biblical scholarship of the last century has revealed more clearly that no single pattern of church order can claim to be apostolic. Many of us in Britain learnt our primary lessons about the union of divided churches from India, where the scale of the missionary task made Christians properly impatient with inherited divisions which had been brought from the West. There is indeed something rather alarming about the expansion of Protestantism, for the particular history of religion which produced our European battles and burnings and bulls, and which developed into our denominational loyalties, has been exported as though part of the divine revelation for all humankind. The painful gymnastics of the Church of England as it related to the new united churches in India reveals the global assumptions of our local history. But the inspiration that came to many of us from India remains. When faced with the question, 'How can we best tackle the evangelization of our society' we too may have to reply that to work in unity is more biblical and more effective than working independently. It is, however, a tough process to overcome long separations and in the United Kingdom this URC experience is the only example to record.

Two of the traditions within this union come from the sixteenth-century Reformation experience in England. Presbyterian church life was inspired by the teaching and practice of Calvin in Geneva and found a small place in English society during the reign of Edward VI, growing in importance during the next century to become one of the main streams of thought during the Civil War. It was a view of the church as a very orderly society, carefully balanced in councils, placing greatest honour in the word of God, avoiding charismatic influences, trusting in elders to work with the ministers for the shepherding of the flock. It saw ministry as God's calling to the whole company and to certain people for special service arising out of that whole, in distinction from those Catholics who saw the priesthood as primary and as constituting the church. So the congregations were linked into presbyteries and those into synods or assemblies in order that there could be mutual supervision and support, particularly in the agonizing times of civil conflict. Although Scottish Presbyterianism had a strong influence, particularly through a southward drift of people, the English variety had its own origins and ethos.

Congregationalism had been born at a more extreme edge of the English Reformation, as a movement of dissent from established and enforced ways of worship, in a mood of radicalism and a taste for martyrdom. For most of the early independents it was the local meeting of believers, covenanted together and celebrating the Lord's Supper, which was the only valid form of visible church. This meeting was, in the early days, illegal. Many varieties of belief appeared. Obedience to conscience was the justification and the rule. Out of this scattered company of independents who had no single formative leader it took a long time to form any cohesive national body, and it was not until the nineteenth century that the Congregational Union was formed, a union with fellowship purposes only in those early days.

The third strand which entered the URC was a later tradition, stemming from the evangelical revival between 1750 and 1815 which so deeply affected Protestantism in North America and in Britain. Among the leaders of revival were Robert and James Haldane who did much to inspire new independent congregations in Scotland and who influenced Thomas Campbell, a pastor in an Irish Presbyterian church. Campbell moved to North America and there, with his son Alexander, left the stern rules of Presbyterianism to develop what he saw as a more biblical form of church life, emphasizing believers' baptism and the essential calling to Christian unity. The Disciples became an influential denomination in the USA and from there formed congregations in Britain. It was these groups, known in the UK as Churches of Christ, that were involved with the URC, after its formation in 1972.

What impelled the union? First, I would put the long and deep commitment of many lay people and ministers to ecumenism as a general movement and to unity as a command of the Lord. These three denominations were among those most thoroughly affected by Edinburgh 1910 and all that followed it, giving some of their finest people to ecumenical service. Second, there was for a long period an engagement between Congregationalists and Presbyterians, a sharing of conferences and youth work, exchange of pulpits, joint work on social issues, and some co-operative church planting. It was thus not difficult for these two groups to agree that negotiations for a union should take place. Third, there was between these two such a spread of congregations that together

they made sense as a national church. Presbyterianism
had a northern strength and in Northumberland was
the great non-Anglican presence. Congregationalism
was more numerous and had large numbers of local
churches in the south of England, in Wales and in
Lancashire and Yorkshire. Although there was some
overlapping, for example on the Wirral and in London
suburbs, it was not so extensive as to cause alarm.
Fourth, there was in the 1960s and 1970s a sense of
falling numbers of members and so a pressure on the
resources of these fairly small denominations. Eco-
nomy, we were reminded, was from the same root as
ecumenical. All this came together in the negotiating
process.

It is clear from their foundation characteristics that
Presbyterians and Congregationalists, who engaged in
a bilateral conversation, would not find it a simple
matter to agree on a basis of church order. I believe that
the major movement by Congregationalists had already
been made, for most had come to see that indepen-
dency is not enough; they had realized the need to act
together in many ways. Often a large congregation
could be independent. It could pay a minister and
maintain its buildings and send resources for mission
overseas. But the small congregation was not independent. As it could not itself pay a minister, other people
had a say in whether it could call a minister. Oversight
was then given to the poor, freedom to the rich, and
that philosophy satisfied no one. Even when this point
was conceded, a major difference in ecclesiology remained. Is the church essentially the local fellowship, or
is it the whole body which acts nationally? At this point
the union basis attempts to bridge the gap. The local
entity is always referred to as the local church, for it is
the church there, not simply a branch office of the

national body. But it is the General Assembly which is given final authority in matters of dispute and is called to represent the full unity of the church. Acting and living together is not to be a matter of choice or whim, it is the way of life in the Holy Spirit; and that 'together' begins locally but does not end there, must not end there. So in the Basis of the URC the word 'church' is applied both locally and nationally.

Another bridging operation was necessary in the ordering of the local church. Presbyterians had, from the days of the Reformation, ordained elders to be the corporate leadership locally, while Congregationalists had invested far more authority in the meeting of all the members. The resulting mix has not meant a single formula applied everywhere, but in essence it has put the church meeting as the council in which all the major local decisions are taken while the elders act as the pastoral leadership group; but I have noticed that the pre-union emphases generally remain, with the weight of decision being recognizably of one tradition or the other. At another level of church life, the region, the new church instituted a new council, the Provincial Synod. There were two main reasons for this. The proposed General Assembly would not have a place for each local church (there were nearly two thousand of them) so it was thought right to ensure a major gathering regionally where every church would be present. The Congregationalists had for a long time had full-time Moderators, ministers set aside to give pastoral care to ministers and their families and to assist in the movement of ministers from one church to another. The Presbyterians, somewhat fearful of a bishop-type figure who might be a sole wielder of power, ensured that this person would act within and through a Synod, so that authority and oversight would always be both corporate and personal. The risk has been a rather heavy structure for a small donomination.

But it was the entry of the Churches of Christ into the one body in 1981 which posed an even tougher theological debate. They had always been a strongly believers' baptism people, confident that this was the New Testament's principal model. The other traditions entering the URC had been paedo-baptist, with very occasional believer's baptism for those who came to a profession of faith without having been baptized in infancy. This major divide in the whole Christian family has not been easily bridged. There is much weight on both sides. So it was a good starting point to recognize that neither tradition should be lost and therefore neither should be exclusive. This was not, and still is not, an easy road. It means a willingness to recognize both routes towards full membership and participation as valid and available. This entails a rejection of any second baptism and an explanation to parents who bring a child for baptism that an alternative is a thanksgiving service with the baptism left until the child is grown and enters faith. Both routes are to be available in every local church, but a conscience clause allows ministers to decide if they would prefer another minister to conduct a particular service. While there are still some difficulties in certain places, partly due to the charismatic movement, this two-track understanding has worked surprisingly well. It is a learning process. We shall see whether the conviction that infants are properly received in baptism as the sacrament of God's grace which is given before any response is possible, whether that gains ground in local practice; or whether the conviction that baptism is a sacrament of conversion and witness to faith in the individual becomes more common. We have been given a new opportunity to develop sacramental understanding.

So Christians with very different histories on particular aspects of faith have all changed in order to come together. Words and prayers over many years had proclaimed the goal of unity. The time came when action had to follow, hard though this was for some. In both Congregationalism and Churches of Christ there are sizeable groups which felt unable to change, sure that their historic formulae were fully adequate for Christian obedience. Those partings were sad and will take time to heal. They testify to the limiting factors of change in our Christian institutions, a profound conviction in many Christians that the way travelled is so holy, so true, so beneficial that no other road can be as good. That way of regarding our past is strongly present in Catholic and Orthodox communions, but it lives in Protestantism too, a rather surprising accompaniment to *Semper reformanda*.

To the radical, all ecclesiastical institutions appear solidly conservative, but in fact there are always some paths which can lead to change. The vastness of the Roman hierarchy and apparatus, for example, means that development is possible in parts of it even when the central policy is to be unchanging. Thus under a conservative pope it is still possible to witness considerable exploration in some areas of the church (for example, Latin America), in some orders (for example, the Jesuits) and in some branches of theology such as the relationship with other faiths. Under a reforming pope that large machine can move slowly but with far-reaching effect, even when there is a body of bureaucratic resistance. The reality of change in institutions always starts with people, perhaps one person, who perceive the calling of God, the transformation of human society, the inadequacy of our present witness to the Lord, the breadth of Christian fellowship and the hope of the kingdom. If we believe that God always is doing a new thing in the world, then we must be open to the voices which proclaim his activity and the human response through newness in our institutions.

7

Officers of the Household

On a gloriously sunny day in the spring of 1982 we sat in a gracious room of the deanery at Canterbury to discuss ecumenical matters with the pope. This followed an inspiring service in the cathedral which included the renewal of baptismal vows. In that moment we had been brought closer together because all were confronted by the same calling of the Lord and the same confidence in his authority. During the conversation which followed we put some questions and received diplomatic but encouraging answers. I was fascinated not only by the pope's deft handling of English but by the circle of silent watchers around the room, the entourage from the Vatican, some with lined, mediaeval faces locked tight and barricaded against any Protestant infection. Perhaps they were carefully noting hopeful ecumenical opportunities for the Roman Catholic Church to use as steps to unity in England, but it did not look like that. But suppose a stranger were to look in at the senior finance committee of the denomination or the disciplinary committee, would that appear any more hopeful? The officers of the household all too often take on the colouring of defenders of the institution rather than servants of the crucified Lord.

This is one reason why ministry has proved to be so intractable an element in all church union discussion. Those who see themselves as guardians of tradition are least able to launch out into a new and risky development, and may even regard it as a basic duty to resist what is new. When the new thing challenges the position of the clergy themselves, then the shutters come down. We become as defensive as a trade union but with the added conviction that we are defending the way of God. So it is vital that in discovering ways forward into the next millenium of church witness we should attempt to sort out what is essentially unchanging in the ministry of the church and what must always be open to modification. We shall not all be agreed on the answers, but that the probing is necessary can hardly be doubted. We cannot afford more ecumenical wrecks on these rocks.

Ministry in the church is a gift of God by the power of the Holy Spirit. That is my starting point. It includes all varieties of ministry, every kind of sacrificial service, the teaching and preaching ministry, the healing and counselling ministry, the ministry of sacraments and administration and music. Wherever we recognize human skill and love energized by the Gospel and placed freely at the disposal of the people of God, there we recognize a gift of God for ministry. In his letters Paul wrote about the diversity of gifts which enable a diversity of callings all directed to the upbuilding of the church and the spreading of the gospel in the world. The root of all these ministries is the life and teaching of Christ, who recognized that the way of the servant was the way of salvation. 'Not to be ministered unto, but to minister' was the whole tenor of a life which was to be given 'as a ransom for many' (Mark 10.45). The Fourth Gospel records the same message attached to the footwashing at the last supper. 'Then if I, your Lord and Master, have washed your feet, you ought also to wash one another's feet' (John 13.14). The service offered by

Christ to the people was a teaching, eye-opening, healing, challenging, forgiving, renewing ministry, calling many into a new relationship with the Father and thus into new understanding of each other, promising that life which is of the spirit, trusting always in God's love. Our ministries reflect that witness, fitfully, partially, but they have no other foundation. Here is the eternal quality of Christian ministry, that it follows the way of Christ and thus reveals the eternal nature of God. This is our greatest claim and most daunting test, for by this we are measured.

But Christ was the outsider, not of the priestly family, unrecognized by the temple authorities, the wanderer who could only make himself known to his followers by analogy and dialogue and sign. Those of us who minister in the church cannot follow the same road for we are set safely within a community and often are given the honoured seats. We are the insiders. There is a risk here that the service to be offered has been so transmuted by the corporate life of the church that lordship becomes the regular mode and footwashing the very occasional corrective. The risk is all the greater in hierarchical and authoritarian churches.

Jesus Christ not only was an outsider but sought others on the edges of society, the lepers both physical and moral, so that the shepherd looking for a lost sheep became a most natural picture of his ministry. We are all too often so wrapped up in our essential ministry to those within the fold that we can hardly spare time or energy to befriend people of no faith, who are battling with life in the hard places of the world. If we are to reflect the way of Christ, then we have to be critical of the inward-looking church which may demand a self-absorbed ministry.

The abiding sense of Christ's teaching is that he

pointed away from himself towards the Father, whose way for humanity or whose reign was the primary sermon preached, and whose forgiveness to the penitent was proclaimed and whose generosity and faithfulness were revealed at every turn. So the ministries of the church are not primarily directed towards the glory of the church, or even its growth, but first of all towards enabling men and women to know the reality of God. Anything that intrudes on that objective has to be examined very critically. Diversions come to us in many ways. Some of the devotion to social concern, which always must be part of Christian witness, may be an alibi for those who cannot speak of God; or a ministry to the sick may be an evasion of healing the broken spirit. In the same way a ministry directed towards church discipline, order, and strength may begin to replace the living God with an idol.

The ministry revealed in Christ is one where word and action are unified. There have always been plenty of preachers with wonderful words. The world is never short of them. Jesus came to be a witness to God, to live out the divine life and to demonstrate God's love, so that the claim to be the way, the truth, and the life was justified by the evidence. So ministry in the pattern of Christ is never concerned only with correct teaching or performing of rituals. It is also about ways of life that are faithful to the gospel and reflect, in a very imperfect way, what God is doing in his world. Ordination is a commitment to such a life.

In these ways the eternal character of God's calling becomes known to us. The far more controversial issue (though not a deeper one) is whether the forms of ministry are as constant as its character. Are the forms given to us by God in the ministry of Christ, or are they given by special revelation to the developing church, or are they essentially variable responses to the context in which ministry is exercised? This is one of the critical questions which lies between catholic and reformed traditions of churchmanship. On the one side, faith and order are rolled up into a single package of obedience to the Lord; on the other they are separable, different orders of knowledge and not to be confused. I belong to the second company and argue for that position, but I hope also recognizing the weight and the loyalty that constitute the first.

In the Final Report of the Anglican-Roman Catholic International Commission there is a revealing passage on priestly ministry.

> The priestly sacrifice of Jesus was unique, as is also his continuing High Priesthood. Despite the fact that in the New Testament ministers are never called 'priests' (*hiereis*), Christians came to see the priestly role of Christ reflected in these ministers and used priestly terms in describing them. Because the euchar-ist is the memorial of the sacrifice of Christ, the action of the presiding minister in reciting again the words of Christ at the last supper and distributing to the assembly the holy gifts is seen to stand in a sacra-mental relation to what Christ himself did in offer-ing his own sacrifice. So our two traditions commonly use priestly terms in speaking about the ordained ministry.[1]

The points that interest us here are the words 'came to see' and 'use priestly terms'. It is surely true historically that Christians 'came to see' ministers in the style of priests, but this argues that a change had occurred after

[1] *Ministry and Ordination: Statement*, 13 in ARCIC, *The Final Report*, SPCK/CTS 1982, p. 35.

the New Testament period, a change happening for
many reasons, good and bad, and a change which itself
could be subject to amendment. They came to see
ministers as priests largely because this was the universal pattern of Roman pagan religions and of Judaism. It
was as priests – and sacrificing priests – that religious
leaders were known, guardians of the shrine, holders of
the wisdom, separated for a sacred purpose. The association with the High Priesthood of Christ was only one
dimension of this popular pressure. It is therefore
possible that in 'coming to see' ministry in terms of
priesthood Christians were influenced by the religious
context and so misinterpreted the essential qualities of
apostolic ministry. But this is where the emphasis lay in
catholic tradition, and we all have to learn how to
respond to it constructively. This is why the other
ARCIC phrase is interesting. 'Our two traditions commonly use priestly terms' is only partially accurate, for
in using the terms very many Christians in the catholic
tradition have come to understand and to practise
ministry as priesthood. The terms have in fact often
dictated the theology. The whole trend has been to
develop, in catholic church order, a priesthood with
authority and powers like those of the ancient pagan
priests, and to fight against that has been hard for
reformers within and critics without. Having witnessed
a historical process of assimilation the church then
rested upon the result as though this was the divine
intention for every age, not to be seriously questioned.
But the questioning today is vital. If there is to be
reconciliation of ministries then we have to come closer
in our understanding of the essential quality of God's
gift and calling, and on the basis of New Testament
evidence it would seem that 'priesthood' is not the
major factor in apostolic ministry. It is one way of

looking. But it has never been the only way and is probably not the most essential to the continuing witness of the church to Christ.

The priest, however, has never been the sum total of the ministry of the church. All the modern documents wrestling with the forms of Christian ministry refer to bishop, presbyter/priest, and deacon as the most commonly accepted forms through the centuries, thus comprising a three-fold pattern which neatly reflects the trinitarian understanding of God. Here again the history in the early period of the church shows development, with much confusion as to the precise ordering of ministry during the first century and with later assimilation to the very class conscious society of the Roman empire. There was never any suggestion that Jesus had set down this three-fold pattern of ministry as his instruction for the disciples. It was a historical development. The WCC Lima text puts it this way:

> The New Testament does not describe a single pattern of ministry which might serve as a blueprint or continuing norm for all future ministry in the Church. In the New Testament there appears rather a variety of forms which existed at different places and times. As the Holy Spirit continued to lead the Church in life, worship and mission, certain elements from this early variety were further developed and became settled into a more universal pattern of ministry.[1]

Precisely because this was the way it happened we should be safe against all attempts to give to the one form an essential, normative character. This is not to say that the model has been a bad one or has failed to carry

---

[1] WCC, *Baptism, Eucharist and Ministry*, Faith and Order Paper No. 111, p. 24.

forward the ministry of Christ. That would be patently
untrue. Those who have accepted ordination in the
three-fold pattern across the centuries have revealed
within it great strengths and possibilities. But that is a
very different thing from claiming it to be the one divine
pattern for all time. A historical development then may
be matched by a historical development now. The
second and third centuries AD had no monopoly of
spiritual insight, nor of leadership models.

The Lima text goes on to set the historical pattern in
the whole unity process.

> Although there is no single New Testament pattern,
> although the Spirit has many times led the Church to
> adapt its ministries to contextual needs, and although
> other forms of ordained ministry have been blessed
> with the gifts of the Holy Spirit, nevertheless the
> threefold ministry of bishop, presbyter and deacon
> may serve today as an expression of the unity we seek
> and also as a means for achieving it.[1]

This is a very careful ecumenical sentence which hinges
on the verb 'may serve'. In the opinion of many it will
serve and must serve; in the view of others it is unlikely
to serve into the next millenium. But the Lima text is
clear that this model is not to be seen as divine command; it is rather the pragmatic basis on which greater
unity may be achieved because no other pattern secures
such wide acceptance. So the question posed to all
churches which do not have a three-fold ministry is
whether greater unity and universality can be secured
in this way, and whether the pattern holds sufficient
flexibility to serve the gospel in modern society. Does it
confine the ministry of the people of God or release

[1] Ibid.

energy for service? Does it enable the permanent quality of the gospel to shine clearly in an institution which is also a pilgrimage? While I am ready to go a long way to find that ministry which can bind us together, I am aware of the theological tension revealed in the recent debates. This comes very clearly to the surface in the ARCIC Report, where the passage on Christian ministers includes this:

> Nevertheless their ministry is not an extension of the common Christian priesthood but belongs to another realm of the gifts of the Spirit.[1]

If we believe that the fundamental ministry is that of the whole church as the servant of Christ the servant, and if we believe that the Holy Spirit gives abilities and voices and courage and love to all who pray in faith, then this is a divisive and unhelpful way to speak of ministry. There is only one realm of the gifts of the Spirit, the realm of God's grace. So if we in the Reformed tradition are led towards three-fold ministry for the sake of a universally accepted ministry, then it cannot be on the assumptions which appear to lie behind the ARCIC Report. If such assumptions are vital to those in the catholic tradition then the gap has not been bridged by the great BEM enterprise, and a long journey into the fullness of God's truth remains.

The gap becomes very evident when the ordination of women is debated, as it must be throughout the world church. In my own tradition the debate was concluded seventy years ago when the first woman was ordained to the ministry of the word and sacraments, for no theological question has since been raised on this issue among us. Within the Church of England and the

[1] Op. cit., p. 36.

Roman Catholic Church we sense the hardness of the
issue, the passions that are raised and threats of disrup-
tion filtering to the surface. For the purpose of this essay
the aspect of the debate which is important concerns the
permanence or otherwise of a male ministry.

For one of the catholic arguments which has been
pressed (for example by Graham Leonard, Bishop of
London) is that the incarnation of God in Jesus Christ
occurred within a patriarchal society, with men as the
chosen apostles, and that this sets the standard for all
future ministry which is called to represent Christ. The
historical fact is there for us all to read. God came to us
as a man, not a woman, and he called first to him a
group of men. It is worth noting that even in the patriarchal society with men given the key places of authority, the Gospel narratives stress the exceptional place of
women. For example, the declaration of the person of
Christ which Matthew gives to Peter (Matt. 16.16) is
shown in John to have been spoken by Martha, a
housewife of Bethany (John 11.27). All four Gospels tell
us that women were the first witnesses of the resurrection, the first to tell this good news and to lift the
low spirits of the apostolic group. Even so, the male
dominance of that social context is clear. What is very
unclear is why this should be regarded as determinative
for all future church order.

Those who press this case appear to me to have
missed the central reality of incarnation, which is that
God truly enters into the historical process. It was
within that limited world, that imperial context, that
forlorn hope, that decaying pantheon that Jesus came
and lived, accepting those limits on knowledge. This
was involved in being human. But if we then freeze that
context for all time and say 'Because it was so then it
must always be so' we seek to resist the historical

process rather than let Jesus live in it. It is like the fond mother who cannot bear to let her son grow up and insists 'But you always liked Marmite sandwiches.' Or like the former colonial officer who cannot think of his country except through the bugle and the flag at sunset. So we can annul the present reality of Christ in our world by the antiquarian clothes we insist he wears. Yet if it is right to continue for ever in the church the male-dominated society, it is surely right also to retain all the cultural aspects of first-century Palestine. So we should be deeply involved in demon-possession and in attributing illness to spiritual invasions, we should resist all portraits and statues, we should recline in groups of twelve at the eucharist, and rest content with slavery. Yet we cannot do these things. The world has moved on. Our vision and skills and temptations have changed. It is therefore impossible for us sensibly to crave a male clergy and a male-dominated church because the New Testament revelation took place where and when it did. The fact that Jesus was a man has never been taken to mean that God is male, nor has the term Father precluded the motherly gifts of patient care. Jesus was a Jew, but we do not deduce that God is. So we accept that the historical contingencies of the incarnation do not all indicate the eternal character of God. What is true is that God accepted the limitations of the cultural, historical context in order to reveal his nature to us, and still does so.

When we go on to ask how Jesus is physically represented in the world today I cannot see any other answer than that it is by both men and women. He is represented by loving lives, by joyful lives, by healing lives, by burden-bearing lives. Gender has no role there. The saints are not of one gender. Jesus Christ is represented also by every preacher of the Gospel and everyone who presides at the sacraments. Those who have experienced women in these forms of ministry have no doubt that Christ is represented by them. This concept of a man being necessary to convey Christ to us at the central moment of the church's devotion shows a very strange kind of imagination, for the clothing and looks of the minister are usually very far from the wandering Jewish teacher. It is not the looks that convey Christ, not the physical attributes. It is the dedication, the spiritual quality, the truth, the word, the corporate action and prayer, the whole life of a worshipping community in which the minister is part which tells us of Christ alive today.

We need also to face the requirement of continuity, and here some Protestant groups have not been sensitive to the life of the church universal, acting as though ministry belongs only to the here and now. Such spasmodic, local authorization of ministers cannot carry with it the sign of the whole people of God, and may, by its isolationist character, actually deny the universal fellowship. While all ministries are defective in the sense that they do not serve the whole body of Christian people, the aim, even in the divided church, must be to act as fully as possible in a representative way. This is where the house-church movement has often failed to enhance the witness of the mainstream churches, for the local leadership, often authoritarian in style, has had no representative character. A thousand micropopes are no more helpful to the unity of all Christian people than Pius IX was in 1870, when his teaching authority was elevated far above the conscience of the church itself.

Continuity is important because the church needs assurance that those who teach are not making up a new Gospel and so leading people out of the fellowship of Christ. So the selection, training and ordination procedures are carried out by as representative a body as is possible in our present denominational life. This does not mean that what is to be taught may only be repetition of what was taught before; a gramophone would then serve us very well. Each re-interpretation and proclamation of the one Gospel of Christ in the ever-new circumstances of life needs to be based on a knowledge of what has gone before, for the Holy Spirit surely does not indulge in self-contradiction, but in the development of truth and light. It is a cause for gratitude that great responsibility has been shown by denominations which are free to act unilaterally but have chosen to maintain a continuity of ministry, ordained and authorized, as a witness to that wholeness which is God's design for the church.

But this continuity element does come into collision with the radicalism of the Quakers and with movements more recently to omit ordination for a special ministry and regard all committed members as equally ordained. What is continuous in the church, it can be claimed, is not its ministers but its faithful people. They, in all ages and places, are the living testimony to Christ; they hold the apostolic commission. I believe this latter claim is indeed true but that it does not remove the need for a publicly recognized and authorized special ministry of those who give their lives to the service of the gospel in the church. A universally recognized ministry requires a measure of continuity and order and training, for otherwise we are subject to the local and spasmodic influence of those who are self-appointed. The great value of the witness of the Religious Society of Friends is to remind the whole church that, although a regular ministry is needed to fulfil all that the church is called to be and to do, yet the faithful people gathered together for prayer and meditation constitute a valid witness to Jesus Christ and a fellowship of the Holy Spirit. They puncture all exclusivist balloons. They broaden our understanding of the people of God.

They also stand in the sharpest opposition to the catholic claim that the ministry constitutes the church, and is defined by the apostolic succession. The Second Vatican Council expressed this at considerable length, but this brief extract shows the clear trend of thought:

> Just as the role that the Lord gave individually to Peter, the first among the apostles, is permanent and was meant to be transmitted to his successors, so also the apostles' office of nurturing the Church is permanent and was meant to be exercised without interruption by the sacred order of bishops. Therefore this sacred Synod teaches that by divine institution bishops have succeeded to the place of the apostles as shepherds of the church, and that he who hears them, hears Christ, while he who rejects them, rejects Christ and Him who sent Christ (*Lumen Gentium*, 3.20).

So strong a claim would come with more persuasive force if it were not made by the bishops themselves, and if the assumptions were more rigorously tested. With such claims at one end of the spectrum and the Friends at the other, it often seems that the ministry question will forever divide the church. I believe we can only make progress here by returning to the ministry of Christ himself and those qualities which are utterly distinctive and are from God and of God. If those qualities, which I mentioned at the beginning of this chapter, are carried through the life of the church in a way which is orderly but flexible, disciplined and generous, prayerful and not standing on dignity, then the ministry will serve the Gospel. Of course the ministers of the church are very imperfect, both in understanding and in character, and therefore absolutist claims for them can have no universal assent. The guarantor of Gospel truth is not the minister, the bishop or the pope, but always the Holy Spirit. The Spirit is not to be defined in terms of our institutional framework but is free to come like wind and fire, filling the house and creating, by faith, officers of the household to serve humanity. Our challenge is to recognize that gift in such ways that all the household may rejoice.

8

Sing a New Song

It is one of the most general presuppositions of religious people that the instinct of worship is universal. When we delve into early human history we find evidences of worship, and there is no continent where worship has been absent altogether during recorded history. So we deduce the general principle. It is indeed supported by the stubborn character of worship in places where powerful authority would stamp it out – as in the Cultural Revolution in China or the 1917 to 1970 period in the Soviet Union. In a mood of questioning we could place against that the evidence of western Europe where the majority of people declines to participate in public worship, and probably has no habit of private worship either. Has worship frequently been a minority experience even in religious ages? It is hard to judge, but the British figures in the mid-nineteenth century (a nominally religious period) indicate that less than half the population went to church regularly. So it is probably safer to say that the instinct to worship is widespread but is often overlaid by tough strata of indifference or of other preoccupations.

Christian worship, therefore, has caught hold of something deep in the human psyche, pointing beyond the narrow limits of sight, touch, hearing, deducing, cataloguing to the immeasurable arena of the spirit. It testifies to the eternal dimension in our make-up. Those who, in worship, are 'caught up in the heavenlies' or are given 'moments of disclosure' break through one of the limits of our mental apparatus. Worship has other purposes than this – the binding together of the fellowship, teaching the Bible, offering up our scarred lives and world to the Saviour, making a public witness to the dimension of the spirit within a secularized society – but that sense of the beyond in the midst is the nearest we come to a holy of holies in the Christian pilgrimage.

Such awareness cannot be programmed, and for that we are grateful. The infinite variety of personality, expectation, taste, knowledge, attitude, upbringing, and insight means that the deep joy of worship touches us in a thousand different ways. If it were not so then we would be subject to a spiritual rigor mortis, one route to be followed by all with one conclusion guaranteed. Some forms of Islam have come close to this and have been accompanied by a totalitarian dominance over human life which contrasts strangely with the freedom which God gives to his creation. We are becoming aware in many fields of the pluralism that appears to be written into the constitution of human life. Therefore we can delight in the diversity of worship. The appeal has to be as broad as human culture. The language of worship has to contain every human language, not only languages in the usual sense but also the language of colour, design, movement, music, poetry, for there are some who speak to God and hear God most clearly in such forms. There is no single prescribed route to spiritual understanding, yet there are some constants which we recognize through all the variations. Chief among these are the word and the sacraments. All Christian worship from the earliest days has rested on these two reference points, although the balance between them has differed sharply. Are these the permanent elements for all worship everywhere if it is to be worship of God through Jesus Christ? And may all the rest be developed anew in every generation?

I believe any such distinction is too facile. That there are these two constant elements throughout Christian history is plain, but there are others equally widespread, for example the act of confession, the prayers of intercession and the chanting or singing of praise. Just as we are given no constitution of the church in the New Testament so we are given no order of worship either, but there are plenty of hints in the Acts and Epistles that all these elements were present. At times, according to I Corinthians, the orderliness of worship was overcome by pentecostal enthusiasm and by ignorance about the way to share the holy meal. Informality and variety would seem to be characteristics, with the apostles' teaching as a dominant feature whenever they were present. The word – at first that oral tradition and then later the use of written texts – focussed the event of Christ for the hearers, persuading them that this was the promised salvation from God, while the sacraments were public participation in that gift of God, a binding to Christ and to his people. The permanent, unchanging factor throughout is the gift of God in Christ. That is the cause of celebration and the subject matter, the basis of the Christian festivals and the heart of preaching; it is the ground for the people's approach to God in prayer and praise. God has come to us. This is the form of his coming. This is his self-offering and this is his victory. This is God with us and for us. Receive him, trust him, follow him, learn from him and we will be joined to him for ever. That is the confident ground on which worship has been built in every tradition; it is what is given to us and not what we have made; and it is that basis which is confirmed in our hearts by the continuing gift of the Holy Spirit.

If that basis is secure then infinite variation is possible in the actual ordering, style and language of worship. But, the critical question has to be asked, how do we made the basis secure? Is it not wise to secure the essentials by setting down one liturgical form which everyone will use, so that only the best model is used and even the most untrained Christian may receive the full diet set down in the most beautiful language? Why risk the deviations which may lead us away from the unity of the body of Christ? This is one of the great ecumenical questions which lies between the Christian traditions, and I cannot respond as an independent observer for I have participated all my life in one of the traditions.

So my response is that although a prescribed, uniform liturgy has great values it is also a risk, and often a high risk, for spiritual life. The values are unquestionable. Regularity, continuity, beauty, theological comprehensiveness – all that is deeply-rooted help to the worshipper. In times of sorrow, loneliness, or persecution that written liturgy may be a precious gift, as full of meaning as the New Testament itself. Where clergy are scarce, or have little training, the book provides resources from the wider church. Those of us who have traditionally resisted a prescribed liturgy also need to give thanks for all that it has given to the people of God in both Eastern and Western traditions. The risk, however, is considerable. The liturgy readily becomes an antiquarian study, a delight in the poetry of another age, as the sporadic defenders of the old Anglican prayer book and the Latin mass reveal. It may in fact become a charm bracelet, a totem, so that we believe it is only possible truly to worship God in old phrases, in old robes, in old buildings. Such passionate attachment to one lovely approach to God then prevents the worshipper from developing a contemporary way of prayer. We always have to worship in other people's words because we have none of our own. Silent Christians may be those who are utterly dependent on the language of tradition. It is a risk. Another is that the prescribed form will itself be given a permanence it does not deserve and so come to rule the church rather than serve the Gospel. Yet the liturgy, even the most magnificent, is a way of response to God, made up of human words and subject to human limitations. Even though we call it the Divine Liturgy, because of its depth or beauty or antiquity, it belongs to the history of human response to the Word made flesh, and did not descend with the angels. The third area of risk is that the conscience or individuality of the believer may be suppressed, for the assumption behind prescribed liturgy is that everyone who follows Christ can approach God in the same way. One road can suit all travellers. This is obviously not so. The determination that there be only one way of worship then effectively ensures the division of the church, for the variety of human response to God cannot be diminished by prescription. It is significant that even in countries where there has been an overwhelming majority of Orthodox or Catholic Christians the varieties of Protestantism still exist, tough minorities that have their own appeal to the human heart. The human spirit cannot be confined to a single track.

Yet development in contemporary styles and in many local cultures could easily lead to varieties of worship which are so idiosyncratic, so personal and transitory that they fail to carry the weight of the message of the cross. I do not mean that every Christian act of worship necessarily holds within it a total statement of the Gospel, for that would be overwhelming, but the danger of shallow emotionalism is that it satisfies no one but the author. The warnings of Paul in I Corinthians 14 still need to be heard, for he recognized the eventual futility of individual outpourings which failed to transmit the content of the Gospel. All the diverse gifts of the Spirit 'must aim at one thing, to build up the church' (14.26). Between an authoritarian prescription and an individual outpouring, between Archbishop Lefèbvre and Caribbean pentecostals there are many middle ways which declare the essence of the gospel in the words of everyday and the images of eternity.

It is that note of eternity and wonder that is clearly most at risk in the modern adaptations of worship in each human culture. As we concentrate our energies on the immediate struggles of life, which we are bound to do, and become absorbed in the things that money can buy, which is our contemporary weakness, so we lose our sense of awe before the great mysteries and powers of the God who gave life to the cosmos. There is some relation between the otherness of God and the poetic distance of the liturgy, a matter very hard to diagnose but recognizable to many. To speak of the glory of God in the language of the tabloid press is like attempting haute cuisine based on chips with tomato sauce. So we look for a poetry of praise which will both make vernacular sense, being words we can honestly say from our hearts, and lift our spirits beyond the horizon of our eyes. It was such a language which, two centuries ago, found a voice in Watts, Doddridge and the Wesleys and now is heard in many contemporary hymn writers. Where the aim is only to be contemporary, we fail; it is to seek a way of approach to God which reveals the eternal light in the flickering torches of our lives. That is when we are led, as a congregation, to adore the wonder of the redeeming Lord.

But even that last phrase is inadequate by itself. To

wonder and adore is, I believe, at the heart of worship in all the great religions, and if we have lost that attitude then it is doubtful whether we can rescue worship in our generation. There is, however, another note which has to be sounded, that of participation. We all know of worship which invites the worshippers to be an audience, to watch from afar as the actors go through the ritual, dressed in splendour and attendant on the mysteries. That style has belonged to cultures where priests have been the only educated people, or where the theology fixes on ordination to the priesthood as the only passport to the central mystery of Christ's presence. That points, perhaps, to the Orthodox experience. But the very same style has been well known in the nonconformist churches when famous preachers took a place very similar to great actors, impressing the crowd with eloquence, raising a laugh with their stories, frightening the guilty and calling for applause in the size of the offering. That is a caricature, for it omits all mention of motives and content. There is something real, however, in the risk of turning a congregation into an audience, and thus inviting an 'I-am-not-involved' mentality. They perform and we listen. The central movement of Christian worship has always been two-sided, the action of God and the active response of people to that action. Such response is not only our wonder and praise. It is also our reformation, redirection, commitment of life and resources, our love towards the handicapped in life's race and our resistance to the forces of evil. This whole-hearted response is focussed in our prayers and is largely formed in us through worship. The way it is translated into life will vary in every human culture, but the gift of God which calls the response from us is the great unchanging origin and theme of all Christian worship.

Thus no reform of worship begins with a blank sheet of paper. Already written is our personal experience, that of our fellowship, our communion and the history of worship across the ages. Such a weight of past experience is our guide to what Christians have discovered to be important, it is not a directive from the Lord. Where the latter is handed down to us we recognize the centrality of holy communion in all the traditions except those of the Friends and the Salvation Army. If we enquire into the form of holy communion we are led both to the early, undivided church and its worship, a field deeply dug over by scholars and so widely known, and to the growing consensus among the major churches today. At a recent conference for the ecumenical movement we were invited to worship at daily communion, and on the three days these were Roman Catholic, Church of England and Church of Scotland. Although the details were varied, for example the robes worn and the hymns sung, the basic structure was identical and many of the words used were the same. It is not a long journey for the liturgy to be interchangeable. An attempt at such a broadly-accepted text was provided by the Faith and Order Commission of the World Council of Churches in association with the Lima text, and this was used at the World Council of Churches Vancouver Assembly. I believe the churches are not yet ready to adopt that text, but it was a sign that an agreement for our generation is probably attainable. But what are we to say regarding those who follow Christ but do not participate in the sacraments? Too long they have been downgraded in the theological discussion. They are saying that to begin with a blank sheet of paper is almost possible and that a design of worship must be right for our consciences rather than for continuity with tradition. There can be no doubt as

to the value of the distinctive witness of the Religious
Society of Friends and the Salvation Army as they
preserve a flavour of spirituality which enriches us all.
That the Spirit of the Lord has given them both dynamic
origin and steadfastness and love seems to me sure. But
I do not believe that such a truncated or lopsided
worship can stand as a full experience of the calling of
the church, and so there is always a question of the
'churchly' character of these bodies. If they could be
seen rather as 'orders' within the whole church then I
believe they would serve us all, the Friends offering the
meditative way to God and the Salvation Army offering
the disciplined social witness which is needed in tough
situations around the world. We need this diversity of
approach if Christianity is to be truly available to all, but
our hope must be that in making a specific contribution
there is no schism, and the concept of an 'order' has
been one historical method of effecting this. Our un-
resolved problem is how such an expression of particular emphasis may live within Protestantism, may be
held in honour and may be nourished, as an order can
be in the unitary life of Catholicism. This is to retain the
sacramental centre of worship as the faithful tradition of
the apostolic church and the departures from it as
emphases which never supplant or deny that centre.

Yet even within the sacramental form there is always
the possibility of development, for the details of administration are not given by Christ, nor by the apostles.
History shows both theological development in many
directions and practical changes. The shift from presi-
dent to priest is one of the most dramatic. It is ironic that
those who hold most strongly to a priestly understanding of the minister presiding at the sacraments are also
those who plead for the unchanging tradition, forget-
ting that they give their allegiance to a radical shift from

New Testament theology. And if that one, why not others? The long and fruitless arguments about the transformation of the elements, the nature of their being the flesh and blood, and the power of the words of consecration, all this vast storehouse of disputation, built on erudition and not a little prejudice, has done little to affect the spiritual reality in the lives of Christian disciples. It is as though Christ patiently suffers our arguments, hears all our words, and still gives himself to the humble and penitent heart. Whereas the theological dispute is often about nouns and adjectives, the faith of Christians is sustained by the verbs – we offer, praise, remember, dedicate, share, eat, drink, bless together, and it is the action which speaks to us of Christ. If the doing of the sacramental action is faithful to the New Testament, then variation can be accepted.

In my experience the most noticeable variation was in some of the Polynesian islands where I worked, and where neither bread nor wine was available. Could there be a faithful holy communion? If this is indeed the central act of Christian worship, then it must be possible everywhere. So the elements were food growing locally. For bread we used the pith of the sprouting coconut, which has a texture like Madeira cake, and for wine the milk of the young coconut. Of course some of the imagery of the communion is lost in the translation, but there is also gain, for the simple daily food becomes the holy food and what is ordinary becomes a blessing. Nothing could be more true to the sacramental principle. Such variation seems to me entirely faithful for it enables the focal event to take place in a language that is understood. To have said in those islands, 'No communion service may take place unless and until we can import some Australian wine' would have been to separate worship and life, and to make the cultural context of Palestine formative for a wholly different society.

Nor is it essential for all the elements of Christian worship to be present on every occasion. A great many Christians in the traditions of the Reformation find much of their joy in worship at non-sacramental services. Praise and prayer make up a large part of the diet for some, preaching for others. For some, a personal act of confession is the necessary first step. There are others for whom music is a vital part of worship, without which a service is dry as dust. All this is not to be prescribed, for the infinite variety of human approach to the mystery of God is part of his lovely creation. Indeed, my travels round the churches have made me wish for greater variety than in practice exists. Parts of the world church with a British point of origin are still frequently tied to a Watts/Wesley hymnody and a hymn sandwich order of worship, dominated by the sermon, when other strengths could be gained by local introductions. Provided the principles are clear on which worship through Jesus Christ is based, then the people of God are to be trusted to express hearts and minds in the forms which mean most to them. This runs counter to the argument that a communion or denomination is defined by its worship; that is what holds it together. It is also in opposition to those who see diversity only in peripheral matters – how many candles and have they got the proper liturgical colour this Sunday. I look for such diversity as is required by our human nature, God-given, so that those who long for silence may find it while those who rejoice in fortissimo noise may have that, and those who need pageantry may see it and those who need intellectual stimulus may hear it. All will have a place in the one church of Christ. We need to prefigure that richness in the church life of today.

The over-arching principles which do not change are the Lordship of Christ who is to be trusted and obeyed, the presence of the Holy Spirit who alone enables us to pray as we should, the total inadequacy of our human offering to God and yet his loving acceptance of what we lay before him, the endless liveliness and challenge arising from the Bible, and the vividness of water, bread and wine to bring into our lives the very life of Christ. The forms in which these glimpses of the divine are celebrated belong to the historical context of the disciples of Christ. They have changed and must change if we are to offer our best in worship. Those who trust wholly to one historical pattern of worship have every right to do so for themselves (although the choice of historical period is often a matter of taste rather than truth), but no right to impose their preferred pattern on the whole church of God. This is a very nonconformist view and I confess my inability to present the case for the Orthodox with equal strength. I see a vague, distant beauty but I have never yet found it to be a route which I can follow with intelligence and commitment; that it is so for others, for hosts of believers, I acknowledge with wonder.

9

St Patrick's Breastplate

Most of the consideration so far has been focussed on the character of Christianity and the church as a continuing witness. At this point I turn to the individual experience of faith. None of us comes to Christian faith as a new-born babe in a pristine, untrammelled world, so we all have some relation to the history of faith. But what is that relation? Are we items in a series, which logically follow each other? Are we planets on varied orbits around one sun? Are we organically connected to all other believers or only to the present fellowship we know? What am I in relation to Christ and to the church?

The question becomes more vivid when the charismatic movement enhances individual experience, and often connects the individual with a very small group of like-minded people. Then it may appear that here is a mushroom growth, spawned by the Holy Spirit, unconnected with the soil. The small group may come to see its separateness as its holiness, while affiliation to the historic churches is counted as a falling-away from the urgent grace of God. Such movements are difficult to hold in full fellowship, yet their testimony to the Lord who changes lives is never to be dismissed. So they present a question mark in our ecclesiologies.

Another development which touches many of us is the mobility which sets people free of their Christian associations and enables them to form new attachments. It is now rare for a young person to look forward to a lifetime in membership of one local church. In my own denomination we have enjoyed the custom of giving a little mark of appreciation to those who have been in one local church for sixty years, and the number is not large. As people move, and as they feel free of old denominational prejudices, so each local congregation becomes a more mixed community, with several traditions brought together. In such a case, is the individual choice now king and the local church now on the supermarket shelf? It is a daunting thought to all who cherish the church as the united fellowship given by the Spirit.

Indeed, this issue presses precisely because individualism in religion has become axiomatic in western societies. There are still places in other cultures where being a member of the village or tribe means to be part of its faith pattern and its corporate worship. I think of Samoa as an example. But even there, in comparative isolation, with a very tough corporate understanding of faith and a strong tradition of tribal authority, individualism of the western sort is breaking in and the denim-clad young on motor scooters can zoom past the church service. The mediaeval synthesis is a broken pot, not to be restored, and the spirit of individual choice and conscience has leapt out. Yet we know, if we think of these things at all, that Christianity is not a wholly new beginning with each believer, nor is the individual to be regarded as an isolated speck floating in space, for there is a corporate and continuous body to which each is joined. If the images of the vine and the body and the temple mean anything then they must lead us to have confidence in the binding-together of the members, and if the gift of the Spirit is fellowship or communion then we cannot claim the Spirit's presence while we shun the church. So, in our generation, we are caught between two convictions, that the individual decision, choice and judgment are supreme, and that Christian faith means participating in the total body of believers; caught between the salvation offered by grace to each one and that kingdom-blessing which is only known in a community. No longer can we sink ourselves in a society or fellowship without thought for its tradition, as though the only role for the individual is acceptance and surrender.

As this tension stretches our lives as Christians, we return to the biblical witness and discover that the same tension is present though worked out in very different language from our own. There is a great weight placed on the tribe. To be part of the tribe was a major element in human identity for the people of the Old Testament. There was little sense of personality apart from that, and salvation could only mean health, safety, peace, and prosperity for the tribe. So the 'royal psalms' have their place as songs not just for one leader but for the people too. A permanent part of worship was the act of remembering the tribal history, re-enacting it in song and sign. God has so dealt with us as a people that we sing of salvation. Although that is the very major emphasis, the individual was never wholly forgotten. So the foreigner who settled among the people of Israel was not to be treated as alien, the widow and orphan were to be cared for, Naomi and Ruth were individual personalities, and David could be accused not for neglecting the tribal future but for shameful cruelty to an individual in order to possess his wife. This awareness that there is more to identity than belonging came to its greatest public expression in the ministry of Jeremiah who spoke of a new covenant which would not be a

corporate binding-together, but an individual knowledge of the Lord (31.31). To many in Israel this must
have sounded almost like treason to the family and
tribe, for how could there be a whole-hearted binding
together if each individual were free to make a solitary
peace with God? Jeremiah's vision was fulfilled in the
life of Christ, for there the new covenant was signed on
the cross and there the appeal was made to the individual to enter the kingdom-life. It could appear as
though the corporate identity was under most severe
threat, which is one aspect of the official opposition to
Jesus, but there was also an appeal to a new Israel, a
new bonding, a tribe of the Holy Spirit, a salvation
which would be effective in the world as the household
of faith. The followers of Jesus, in pendulum fashion,
swing between these two dimensions of faith. We know
the very personal appeal and response, which we
signify in believers' baptism, and the corporate belonging to Christ as part of the family, which we lift up to
God in infant baptism. Both dimensions are necessary.
We are not isolated atoms to be rescued by God and to
float for ever in lonely glory, nor are we pew-fodder, to
be engrafted willy-nilly into the continuous institution.
The tension is needed because human nature contains
both dimensions and Christ lifts both to God. If one is
pressed and the other ignored, we see caricatures of
Christian faith. The great Reformers, in pressing the
individual path of faith, were very conscious of the risks
involved if people pushed too far that way and therefore, with reluctance and sometimes with undue sever-
ity, they resisted the more extreme pietists of their day.
So today the charismatic revival movement will only
feed the people of God and serve the great mission of
Christ if it is allied to a corporate awareness of the
church, continuous through history, and present in

every nation. In the same manner the great corporate
institutions of Christianity will only bring light to the
world as they rejoice in individual diversity and accept a
great variety of approaches to the mystery of Christ. A
monolith is a dead thing; but a handful of sand is not
very dynamic either.

It has often seemed to me that the most mature
Christians I have known have been people fully aware
of tradition, nurtured in it, but also transcending it.
I think of a Polynesian pastor who was steeped in island
lore and language and who was as convinced a Protestant
as any, but who was able by grace to leap over all the
barriers of ancient prejudice to befriend and embrace a
lonely Catholic priest. Or a learned theologian who, to
us students, seemed omniscient yet who, as an evangelist, could mount the soapbox in a busy street and
appeal in the simplest of words. Or a leading Catholic
layman who knows the tradition as well as any, who yet
can say, 'Priestly celibacy is a nonsense; no foundation
in scripture whatever.' Such people bear witness to a
tension which, if lived out in faith, is creative.

There is a new birth in each Christian as spiritual life
is given, the beginning of Christ's indwelling by which
we are slowly and imperfectly formed afresh to be like
him. This means endless possibilities, just as each
physical birth has limitless potential. It is new. There is
no repetition. We are not carbon copies. My experience
and perception is unique as yours is, and therefore we
cannot lay down rules or tramlines for the growth of the
spiritual life. Yet it would be extraordinary arrogance in
me to claim that I am the first Christian and have no
need of the history of faith. All that has been given by
God to previous generations helps to form my understanding, just as the Christians of the second generation
depended for their knowledge of Christ on the apostles

and the group around them. It is as though the seed of individual faith is clothed with the colour and texture of the community. Thus the meaning of the cross of Christ reaches the individual heart and mind with the language and emphasis of a tradition; it is not either an angelic gift from above nor our own logic written on an empty page. We may reject much of the tradition, or develop it or simply accept it, but we cannot pretend it does not exist. It is this individual newness in relation to the whole fellowship of faith that makes tradition a living story, never completed. Christian tradition is not a slab of history, a museum exhibit, codified by church lawyers, but a process in which Christ is known in each epoch and culture. We are contributors. That is why there has to be very serious questioning of the theological and ethical views of a local church or minister outside the mainstream, for the stream itself is being shaped each day and may, by ignorance or wilfulness, run into the sand. 'It is for freedom that Christ has set us free,' wrote Paul to the Christian community in Galatia. The consequence was not, 'Therefore you can travel your own road and make up doctrine as you go along,' but 'Stand firm, then, and do not let yourselves be burdened again by a yoke of slavery' (Gal.5.1).

There is another dimension to the life of faith. Not only do we know ourselves to be individuals in relation to the whole body of Christians through the ages, but also in relation to God. What sort of relationship is that? Are we joined to the eternal as every light bulb is to a distant dynamo, so that we have no life of our own? Is Paul's phrase 'I, but not I; it is Christ who lives in me' to be taken as picture language, a poetical phrase for a mystery or as a realistic description of the psychology of faith? As we receive the promise of eternal life are we already lifted out of the process of time to enter the dimension of the spirit? These are mighty questions which touch the mystery of the faith, and we can only approach them as those who pray that we may live in the light of the Gospel. I am attempting here to make four points in response.

1. The life given to us by God in creation is not destroyed or manipulated by God in the act of salvation. What is given is individuality, self-consciousness and complexity, an extraordinary bundle of thoughts, feelings, interests, prejudices, tastes, reactions, fears, and longings that make up each personality. It is precisely those complex personalities whom Jesus met and loved. So we rejoice to read of the distinctiveness of Mary and Martha at Bethany, the variable moods of Peter, the quiet courage of Joseph from Arimathaea and the passionate devotion of Mary of Magdala. Jesus did not demand that they become one sort of person, one pious order, nor one regiment always marching in step. His gift to them of acceptance and new light and divine love and deep challenge was received according to the personal situation of those he addressed, it enhanced the individual gifts already there and so fulfilled the many different personalities. We cannot presume that in the modern world God seeks to do other than that. The work of grace in our hearts is not manipulative. We remain who we are, subject to the same temptations and rejoicing in the same beauty in our world, but the focus of life has shifted from self-satisfaction and self-fulfilment towards the kingdom's way of sharing. It is comforting to imagine and to preach about the full peace given to our hearts by faith, as oil poured on the breaking waves, but most disciples have to tell a different story, about continuing inward struggle, much searching and occasional times of darkness, with peace as promise and goal. We remain ourselves as we face

the cross, and we are still ourselves when God calls us into the fullness of light.

2. A similar emphasis is made by the constant use by Jesus of the name Father. Many other names for God reveal other aspects of his relation to the world. Judge, Creator, Lord of Hosts all emphasize authority and control. But in using Father Jesus was moving human thought towards a more intimate and understanding relationship in which each person is a precious child, known and cared for but free to leave home. It is not that Jesus ignored the element of judgment. It is there, hard and plain in the Gospels. But it is the Father who judges, not a distant enthroned autocrat who distributes punishment with ease. I am baffled by the great Last Judgment scene on the wall of the Sistine Chapel in Rome because Michelangelo appears to have visualized a Christ who casts people away from him as rubbish on to the dump, an interpretation of God's activity which I cannot square with the word Father. We do not worship a Supreme Supervisor who directs all our steps in life, who pushes us into his way or who speaks through us as a ventriloquist might do. Our relationship of love, and therefore of obedience, is a gift which is only received as we will to receive, it is not imposed by natural or supernatural events. The latch is indeed on our side of the door.

But the word Father does not eliminate the mystery of God. Beyond us in concept or image, beyond us in gender, beyond us in time and space, we say Father but must think of Jesus, the face of God for us all. As we study Jesus Christ and recognize the quality of his life and ministry, and as we welcome him, so we begin to know the eternal Spirit who brooded over chaos and who will delight in New Jerusalem at the end. We begin to know. All that we understand of God is but a beginning, and we do not reach the point of claiming to have attained entry to the glory. We are of the earth, earthy.

3. Despite this we know that in the history of spirituality there are people who have been caught up into the seventh heaven and who have been given vivid, direct awareness of the presence of God. I believe that the experience so reported has varied little with the years and the human cultures, and that the similarity with ecstasy in other religions is marked. Perhaps by aptitude and training, by discipline and prayer, and perhaps through the deep emotional pressures of life, some people look through the curtain which is our human limitation to find themselves participating in the music of the spirit. It is a rare experience. We either write it off as delusion or accept that a dimension of life has become visible which normally is hidden from us. We can only refer to that dimension as the spiritual context of human life, the continuity within which the line of history is written. Yet even in these very occasional glimpses of glory the human mind is the lens and is conditioned by upbringing to recognize particular aspects of holiness. For example, the most notable visions of the Virgin Mary have come to young Roman Catholic girls. I would not deny their gift of seeing, but would relate that gift to the training which has raised expectations.

To build a religious system on these rare glimpses would be like basing all astronomy on the arrival of Halley's Comet. Yet they do lead us back to the resurrection of Jesus which is the great affirmation of faith, for there the followers of Jesus saw with clarity what was not visible to the crowd in the street. The curtain was drawn aside and they knew beyond doubt that this was the same Jesus who had died on the cross. So their day-to-day world was lit by the presence of the world beyond, a light of confidence in that reality which encloses us. It is surely right to be sceptical about visions of the eternal for we easily delude ourselves in order to give weight to our convictions, but the train of events which began with the resurrection persuades us that there is a breaking-in which changes human lives.

4. But that change does not remove our humanity nor our passage along the time line; we do not slip out of this life in order to enter another. What God does for us and in us through Christ he does for *us*, the people we are, the people we remain. Our participation in God is rudimentary; what is assured by faith is fulfilment. We know only the *arabon*, the foretaste, the engagement ring and not the wedding. So our understanding of holiness is just a beginning. The biblical picture of a very holy place at the centre of the temple, hidden from the eyes of the crowd, was surely correct in the implication that the holiness of God is beyond us, but incorrect in the suggestion that priests can come closer to God than simple worshippers. This development in us of the likeness of Christ can be witnessed in many aspects of Christian life, and I note two of them.

The first concerns moral judgments. We believe that our human judgments on what constitutes right and wrong only have sound basis as they are founded on the character of God. That is to say that we only draw near to the reality of what is right and wrong as we reflect the eternal foundation of all the created order, for any other basis is liable to tell us what is convenient or profitable rather than what is right. As we recognize in Jesus Christ the very character of God, so our own knowledge of goodness is based securely. But we never go all the way in that direction for we never know the whole of God, and so we frame our judgments in that borderline area where we know a lot about human nature and development, much about causes and effects, a good deal about sin and death and something of the eternal light of God. This becomes plainer when we consider not the ancient simplicities of murder or theft but a modern complexity such as the moral basis of democracy. The forming of a Christian judgment on whether a parliamentary democracy is particularly 'good' or an autocracy particularly 'bad' does not arise simply by learning of Jesus Christ, nor in studying the tribal government of the Old Testament. We have to use many tools of study and consult many interests if we are to make such a judgment, and even then we shall reach only provisional conclusions. The attempt to declare only absolute moral judgments and, short of that, to say nothing, is elevating human voices to the place of God and so failing to acknowledge the mixture we are. Much is provisional in all human life and there is much exploration and uncertainty on the developing frontiers of our life together, so we need humility as we seek to reflect the mind of Christ for the contemporary scene, and not claim too much. This is hard for Christians to accept, for we all find it much simpler to proclaim an unambiguous judgment issued with churchly authority and therefore to be taught with confidence. It is hard, also, to raise questions when people seek only answers. We can always offer what we believe to be the moral basis for a Christian judgment; what we cannot do is invest that belief with the impermeable cloud of divine authority, unless there is plain New Testament support for the judgment.

A second area where our following of Christ is partial is when we make vows. It is traditional for Christians to make vows before God and the congregation and for the church to regard these as binding for ever, in the same way as we understand God's promises to us are binding

for ever. Thus the vows at baptism or confirmation or
entry into a vocation or marriage have a quality of
eternity about them. They are not just vague intentions.
They are religious acts in which we seek the support of
the Holy Spirit for their fulfilment. Yet, because they
remain *our* actions they may be mistaken. In all the
years that follow it may become clear, for example, that
this person is not at all suitable for the religious vocation, and can best serve God in some quite other way.
We know to our cost that marriage vows can be entered
into with confidence yet be revealed as lacking any
sound foundation for building a family. I do not believe
that this fallibility means that we should never make
vows or promises, for we all need the assurance they
provide in religious and social life. We need every
possible help to be faithful to our best moments. But we
cannot interpret such human actions as being of the
same absolute quality as God's faithfulness; our humanity and limitations mean that even our best moments are
infected with ignorance or self-delusion or lack of wisdom or ambition. So when we make these commitments
of total loyalty and love and life we do so as people, not
as gods, and it may be shown later that we have been in
error. This is why it seems both reasonable and Christian
to permit the re-marriage of divorced persons in church,
for otherwise we create an unforgivable sin or error. By
agreeing to this the church may be accused of encouraging a slipshod public attitude to vows of great weight,
and it is therefore essential that all churches should take
great pains in the preparation of people who wish to
take any life-long vow, and not drift into the position of
facile complicity with all who come.

What then does it mean for Paul to say, 'I, but not I, it
is Christ . . .'? If it is the case that (1) in salvation God
does not destroy our individuality and freedom, (2) God

is revealed to us as Father whose loving heart we know in Christ, (3) even in our visions of God we are deeply influenced by upbringing and local culture, and (4) our reception of the divine Spirit in our lives is always partial, never total, then is not the I always the I? I believe the answer is Yes and that we then have to ask in what manner the individual believer is fused with or indwelt by Christ. The first way of meeting this question is to think that the baser aspects of my life are wholly the work of the human I, but that any good I may think or do is the activity of Christ. If we know ourselves at all well, then we surely confess to the constant inadequacy and error which pervades our lives and the tendency to self-esteem and satisfaction which is with us every day. This is the testimony of the saints. Paul writes of it vividly in Romans 7. But there creeps in a strange dualism if we move on from that self-understanding to declare that all the true, generous, loving things in our lives are not ourselves in action but are the work of another who moves in us. This would produce a 'now it's me; now it's him' perception of life which is not discernable in any evidential way. It would also raise difficulties about the meaning of salvation, if the essential personality remains in the grip of abiding evil.

A second way of approach is to think that conversion and the entry into new life is the beginning of a process in which the believer becomes like Christ so that, by grace, it is as though Christ is active repeatedly in all who carry his likeness. There is plainly truth here because we recognize people in whom this is evident. We are blessed to know them. When their names are recorded as martyrs the church remembers them with joy. When courage and steadfastness, gracious self-forgetfulness and healing peace come near us then we are enriched as by the presence of Christ, however unknown the person may be. There is, however, some difficulty here. What is hidden is any decisive step which is the birth of faith. All depends on the steady process of discipleship, with some of us being good students, others never getting a pass mark. So the relation of the Christian to the Lord might be seen as the prize for good conduct – now, at last you have grown to have an aspect of Christ. Yet this is not our total experience, for sometimes it is the newest Christian who is most like the Lord in complete confidence in the Father. Certainly there is growth in Christ-likeness, but that is not the whole story.

Rather, I would place the emphasis on the gift of the Holy Spirit who is, from the moment faith is born in us, the daily companion who teaches us of Christ, educates our conscience, leads us into truth and brings us gifts of character and wisdom. Faith opens the door of our life to this influence. There is no guarantee about our reception of the Spirit. Our old prejudice or fear may still hide truth from us, as is evident from the host of believing Christians in history who have turned on fellow Christians with bitterness and cruelty. We should make no exaggerated claims. But the divine offer is there. God does make himself available in humility so that this I may be led by the Spirit towards the Thou. Our reception of the Spirit is a very unscheduled process, but we have indications through all Christian history of the kinds of discipline that are helpful. Chief among these is the fellowship of Christians and the corporate worship they celebrate, but closely linked is private study and prayer, together with action to serve neighbours in need. We are enabled to receive, in these ways, what God is always seeking to share with us of himself, and as we receive so our lives are shaped after his pattern. Sometimes that reception is overwhelming and sudden; more often it is slow, gradual and accompanied by periods of uncertainty. God does not manipulate his children, and the wandering child may still wander long after the birth of faith. But the door has been opened. That means that we may receive the gifts of God the Spirit, and God receives us as participants in his eternal purpose of life in loving community.

This binding together has always been better described by the poets than the theologians. Nor is it readily expounded in scientific language. We are conscious that the human personality is very complex, that we never entirely understand another person, and that any action of God is a mystery. We remain always part of the stream of history, subject to all the changes of human society, but in faith we also share in that mystery and claim the promise of the risen Christ.

Christ be with me, Christ within me,
Christ behind me, Christ before me,
Christ to win me, Christ to comfort and restore me,
Christ beneath me, Christ above me,
Christ in quiet, Christ in danger,
Christ in hearts of all that love me,
Christ in mouth of friend and stranger.

The words, attributed to St Patrick, frame the prayer of all who would affirm the binding together of time and eternity. Perhaps the Celtic faith facilitates the expression. Here is another.

When thou turn'st away from ill,
Christ is this side of thy hill.

When thou turnest toward good,
Christ is walking in thy wood.

When thy heart says 'Father, pardon',
Then the Lord is in thy garden.

When stern duty wakes to watch
Then his hand is on the latch.

When to love is all thy wit,
Christ doth at thy table sit.

When God's will is thy heart's pole,
Then is Christ thy very soul.

George Macdonald, 1824–1905

But who is this Christ of faith?

10

Yesterday, Today and For Ever

Among the English poets few were as storm-tossed as John Donne, who knew the passionate upheavals of loves and hates, the tensions of aristocratic service, the speculations of philosophy, the calling of the church and the uncertainties of politics. It is not surprising that he often speaks to our condition. He wrote one of the *Elegies*, entitled 'Change', on the theme of human love which is inconstant, but leads on to a broader reflection on movement and progression.

> To live in one land, is captivitie,
> To runne all countries, a wild roguery;
> Waters stincke soon, if in one place they bide,
> And in the vast sea are more purifi'd:
> But when they kisse one banke, and leaving this
> Never looke backe, but the next banke doe kisse,
> Then are they purest; Change is the nursery
> Of musicke, joy, life and eternity.

To bring together change and eternity is the exceptional insight of a man who understood both. It provides the text for this chapter. For all too often we have only thought of the eternal as being totally static. If we think of the most long-lasting object we know on earth, a mountain, then we may reflect on the eternal as an infinite mountain, super-Everest which sits and lasts and lasts and lasts. The next step may be to regard as godlike those things which are closest to the image.

It is in this way that I believe the Hebrews text 'Jesus Christ is the same, yesterday, today and for ever' may both teach and strengthen us but may be readily misused to argue the wrong sort of permanence. What we know of God stems from that brief life in the Near East. All our imagining, deduction, praise, theology and devotion spring out of our conviction that that life on earth was a true revealing of the life which is beyond sight. What happened at that point in history is not changeable, for it is part of the record along the time-line. We may have a host of differing emphases as we read the Gospels and teach them and pray them, but we cannot alter what happened. That is for ever the same.

When we believe that Jesus shows us God in a human life we also hold to what does not change, the character of God. It is part of our humanity to be developing and unpredictable as our days unfold. But the eternal God is not a part of the time-line; he encloses, surrounds and sustains history. 'Were you there,' asked the Lord of Job, 'when I laid the foundations of the earth?' (38.4). 'Who has set limits to the spirit of the Lord? And what counsellor stood at his side to instruct him?' asked Isaiah (40.13). Alpha precedes history and Omega concludes it; the Lord of history claims both. So we do not need to envisage any historical development, as we understand it, in God. If we know who he is, if we know him at all, then we know what is, in our terms, of absolute permanence. Jesus in his ministry spoke of the identity of himself and God. 'My Father and I are one' (John 10.30); 'Know that the Father is in me, and I in the Father' (John 14.10). This identity is the ground of revelation; what is seen with the eyes reveals what is beyond sight. Thus we know, in the teaching, actions, attitudes, relationships, death and resurrection of Jesus, the nature of the eternal God, and if we know this at all, we know it for ever. That one shaft of light came from the source of light which is always shining, though we do not see the source through the clouds. It is significant that when the writer to the Hebrews used the phrase, 'Jesus Christ the same, yesterday, today and for ever', he was actually warning about outlandish teachings which were unfaithful to the life of Christ. We cannot, he was urging, invent a new revelation which is different from what we know in Christ. Thankfully this is still the Christian position, that what we have seen of a loving, self-sacrificing, healing, forgiving, challenging and incorruptible God is what is true always and everywhere.

That is the leap of faith, always unprovable in logic but witnessed by the millions who have recognized the light of God in Christ. What, then, is the element of change? It is precisely the reality of incarnation. Jesus came in history, wholly enfleshed at that point and in that land, his approach to human life, to nature and to the universe all of a piece with his contemporaries, his religious foundation that of his people, his language the common tongue, his vision of heaven and hell close to the common mind and his style of ministry familiarly unwelcome to the authorities. All that is unrepeatable and we, at this distance, cannot fully enter into the mind of those who met Jesus face to face. The very words used carry very different connotations in our society, so that when we read 'Behold, the Lamb of God' there is a great leap of translation necessary to carry anything like the same meaning today. By entering human history at one point in a human life God shows all of himself that can be visible to our eyes, yet the understanding and the implications of that life cannot be frozen. If God is speaking to us then it is in our language, for our situation, that we might know his unchanging love. It is the resurrection and the ascension of Jesus that enables the translation to happen, for the Jesus of history became the Christ of glory, available to every culture and generation in the clothes and language that will meet human need. Unless there is such constant translation of the living Word of God then history and the historian claim all the glory and the archaeologist digs down to the divine. But why do we seek the living among the dead? Christ is the living lord who calls us freshly on every page of our lives and does not need a Turin shroud to show us his face. His language is the language of our streets. His challenge is to our compromised institutions and established hierarchies. His healing touch is for our neighbour. His cross-bearing is the weight of our despair. He is the same yesterday, today and for ever as he lives afresh for us to reveal the very same sacrificial love that took him to the cross. The Jesus of history must never become an archaism, so clothed in piety and distance that we escape altogether the pressure of his presence.

All human response to Jesus Christ is partial and in continual development. The totality of the man Jesus is not available to us. The biblical record is but a fraction of the life itself. When the apostles sought the words with which to describe the tremendous liberating power of this man on the cross they stumbled and searched for poetic forms and metaphors just as we have to do, using all that their varied cultures could offer. They are our guides to Jesus and without them we do not know him, but they did not record the whole of the history nor can we presume that they enclosed in their brief writings the totality of his meaning for the world. Authoritative their testimony most surely is, but closed, complete and final are different claims raising other questions. We hold to a historical faith; our salvation came to us in that particular history. Yet history did not stop at that point, and we live in the period when those historical answers do not meet all our questions.

This is simply to press the case that the motto of the church 'Reformed and always to be reformed' applies not only to the structures of the church because it is always marred by sin, but also to the thinking of the church, for that is always clouded by ignorance, and to the devotion of the church which through the ages has reflected our mixed motives. In history we cannot spot an immaculate church. All our understanding of the creation points us in this direction. Not only has the creator given to us enquiring and developing minds which are never wholly satisfied with a closed system or ideology, but the creation itself is a process of constant change. In the fifteen thousand million years of the created universe, no two years have been the same. Always, in every field of physical enquiry, we witness progression, movement, explosive events, growing complexity, instability and uncertain boundaries only with difficulty described in universal laws. Our own earth's history is of this sort, and the tiny fraction of that history occupied by the human story reveals change and development, progression and regression in every field of endeavour. Just as the shape of our bodies has changed over the centuries, so have the horizons of the mind. I am surprised how slowly we recognize the physical changes and treat people over six feet tall as still not normal. A prize should be instituted for the airline which designs economy-class seats to fit the person with long legs. That, as you will guess, is a personal plea. But it is a small illustration of our tendency to treat as stable and fixed for ever what is always changing – the average dimensions of our bodies. So if we look for static symbols of eternity we shall not find them within the cosmos.

The words from Hebrews also mean that as Jesus was Lord then (and the claim was explicit in Luke 6.5 and John 13.13), so he is Lord always. He called for followers, for obedience and for sacrifice, drawing people away from all other forms of worship so that God's authority might be acknowledged and loved. That exclusive lordship demands that we do not create new idols, however respectable they may be; that is, we cannot call eternal what is not, we cannot ascribe all honour and glory to what is human, nor can we contain the mystery of God within the formulations of the followers of Christ. Some forms of Christianity come very close to it. Some of the statues of Mary, for example, generate such extraordinary enthusiasm that they come close to the definition of an idol. Some ways of handling the Bible infuse it with the miraculous properties of God's presence. It is as though we are never contented with the humility of the means by which we are led to Christ, but have to elevate them and sanctify them and, in the end, glorify them rather than the Lord. It is an ancient story. The law was given as a means of leading a people towards the way of God; in the end it became god-like, demanding, apart, holy. Then Jesus had to face it with a much greater claim, for 'the Son of Man is Lord even over the Sabbath' (Mark 2.28). This did not mean that the law was to be denied, but that it should always be treated as a partial expression of the holiness of God.

The coming of Jesus was marked by another sign of lordship, the call for repentance, a turning around, a change of mind. This was John the Baptist's sermon text as preparation for the coming and Peter's call on the day of Pentecost. 'Repent', said Jesus, 'for the kingdom of heaven is upon you' (Matt.4.17). But it was not a word to be used once and then forgotten, as though the arrival of Jesus exhausted the meaning and the need. Wherever Jesus comes, men and women are called to repent; it is a word which lodges in the experience of every disciple on every day of the journey, for we have never kept company with Jesus as we should. 'Lord,' prayed the confident elder, 'keep me from error, for you know I am never going to change my mind.' To be confronted by the authority of Christ and the challenge of his way means that we are constantly having to change our minds and overturn our attitudes. So the church also has to do in all the periods of its life and in all its parts, recognizing that compromise has crept in, structures have ossified, triviality has dominated, prejudice has matured, and fear has stained. If we affirm a static church, given once in perfect form for ever, then not only is it handcuffed in meeting new patterns of human life and thought, but it is unable to know the joy of forgiveness and renewal. Thus the Roman Catholic Church has needed to repent of much cruelty inflicted in the name of faith, the Church of England has had to face challenges on its divorce from the working class at the industrial revolution, and my own Reformed Church community has needed to confess that we too often claimed too much for the purity and truth of one part of the family. Now the time has come to repent of all our exclusivist claims to hold and own the truth. Salvation is the gift of God, the eternal, not the property of the church.

The further affirmation of this is in the gift of the Holy Spirit. If we know Christ as Lord, trust him as Saviour and healer, follow him as God's way for humanity, it is because God himself has led us into faith. This is a mystery. How and why there is a response to Christ in one person and not another, when both have been shown the same vision of God's love, is a matter which psychologists may try to explain but which always escapes us. For the Spirit is God and therefore beyond our definition and control. If there were rules or channels or types of people or liturgical forms which enclosed the Spirit, then we would have moulded God within our world of knowledge. The Spirit is free as the wind. The grandest system cannot contain all the possibilities. So while we may, to avoid chaos and to build a continuing body, codify and legislate, we may never absolutize either the visible institutions of Christianity or the theological descriptions of faith. If we do, we find that the power of the Spirit has leapt over our walls and has brought people to faith in other ways or healed their hearts by an unprescribed music. John Taylor, in his splendid book on the Holy Spirit *The Go-Between God*[1] writes of the 'inconsistency of the various incidents of the Spirit's intervention from the day of Pentecost onwards', and shows how none of the expected rules applies, neither the human channel chosen nor the mode in which the Spirit came. This challenges all our attempts to provide religious security through definitions and religious orders, rather than risk the uncertainties of human reception of God's light and truth.

But what of certainty and security and the firm foundations that we need in the flux of passion, growth, change, and decay? If all the property of the faith, both theological and institutional, may itself be in process of development, how can we be assured of the truth of the Christian way? It is a common question but a strange one. There can be no guarantees of faith that arise outside faith, for if there were then faith itself would be unnecessary and we could rely on our proofs and our

[1] SCM Press 1972, p. 119.

logic. We are greatly helped towards faith by all the markers of Christian history and by all the wisdom of the generations, yet at the end we are given faith by the Spirit as an inner conviction that Christ is indeed Lord. It is a conviction which holds us and shapes our thinking but it is, in human terms, not provable; it is a gift of God. Security resides in the utter reliability of God whose promises to us in Christ are never betrayed and whose love never lapses into impatience or tyranny. No visible system of church or state and no intellectual system can destroy that reliability or add to it; we can only witness to it with all the talents given to us.

But God also witnesses to his care for the creation, for the Spirit is always active in human life, and the word of God, as the Spirit focussed on a human situation, calls us repeatedly to a faith which is responsible in a compromised world. God does not leave us alone, as the wandering Israelites discovered in Sinai. What he spoke to us in the life of Christ is constantly renewed and translated so that the challenge of Christ is always a present day challenge, and those who hear and see and speak that challenge are the prophets for our day. There is no antipathy between word and sacraments, though we may emphasize one or the other, for both are means by which the Spirit enables those feeble elements of language and liturgical action to affirm, confirm and renew our faith that Jesus Christ is Lord, to the glory of God the Father.

The assurance and security of faith is thus the object of faith, the one who is beyond and behind and over and under and within our world. In all the multitude of human responses to the gospel there is the companionship of the Holy Spirit who leads us all towards the very life of God, and who blesses us with convergence as we draw closer to that reality, but whom we never experience in totality, clogged as we are with dirty vision and immature hope. Our limitation is also due to the divided character of the Christian community. It is only 'with all the saints' that we can appreciate the full wonder of Christ. In our divided groups we have selective or sectional understandings, never the whole. This is what makes the ecumenical movement so demanding and exciting, not that we are achieving bigger organizations but that we are beginning to glimpse the family of God with all its diversities and tensions and praises. So we learn the meaning of Christ for other cultures and traditions, and thus realize how culturally-conditioned our own theology has been. By speaking of tradition as limited or provisional we do not imply that it is wrong and leading us astray, but that it is never final or the whole of God's light and truth. There is no finality or perfection or infallibility to be found in our temples, churches, chapels, basilicas, abbeys and cathedrals, our bishops, priests and deacons, our cardinals, popes and metropolitans, our theologians, philosophers, linguists, expositors and archaeologists, our social pioneers and radical spirits and politicians, our Christian lawyers and constitution-makers, our saints, our missionary heroes and heroines, our world Christian communions, our denominational structures, our glimpses of heaven and our ecstatic gifts of the Spirit, our creeds and encyclicals and resolutions and pronouncements, for all are part of the groping and stumbling pilgrimage of the people of faith as they look towards Jesus, the author and finisher of faith, alpha and omega of life.

This is profound cause for thanksgiving. If finality were there, at one stage in the life of the church or in one school of theology, then repetition would be the sum of obedience. We would be, in London terms, on the Circle Line with no destination, seeing the same

stations appearing out of the darkness. In biblical terms
we would be Rechabites, committed to the past, holding
romantic notions of the desert, objecting to any different culture, standing symbols that a tent is the only
real place to meet God (Jer.35.1–11). Yet the terrors of a
world adrift are not to be healed by the sermons of the
past. It is Jesus Christ whose saving love reaches us in
fresh language who is the same; we respond within the
moment which is given to us, to meet the challenge
which comes to us and to no one else. One of the
reasons why Christians have had so little effect in
healing the massive tragedies of our world is that we
have regularly thought of past history as the sacred
model of God's action. Thus many Protestants in Ulster
retain a perception of Catholicism which may have been
justified a century ago, and they form their political
action accordingly, thus freezing out any hope of reconciliation. Many Christians retain a perception of a 'missionary' as though the 1830s are still here and stories of
pioneer jungle treks should enliven the church magazine.
So long as that image keeps its power, new forms of
missionary witness lack understanding and support.
But we are called to share the transforming love of
Christ in this world of space travel, military dictator-
ships, pop music, redundancy, heart disease, Benidorm,
Chinese take-away, divorce, the international manipu-
lation of currency, de-forestation, and television politics.
While history may teach us of the many false steps
taken by Christians and the many splendid actions and
visions too, no history can tell us how to make credible
that man on the cross in our world. We depend on the
gifts of the Spirit to enliven our human skills both in
understanding the forces which shape our world and in
communicating the challenge of the cross.

Christian faith does not transform these temporary

phases of history into eternal cities. The best we can do with all the artistry, craftsmanship, poetry, and philosophy of the Christian community is to put up cardboard shanty towns on the road to the city of God. Of course we pray that they reflect a little of the light and design of the eternal, but they remain transient and immature. The eternal city does not need temples; it is all worship. But we need them in our human pilgrimage in order to make space for worship. Our search for permanent security on earth and our reluctance to trust in the Holy Spirit's leading, and possibly our satisfaction with particular parts of the journey so far, have all led us to treat as unchangeable those temporary stopping places.

There is only one Christ who has spoken to Galilean fishermen and Roman soldiers and American marines and Australian cricketers and Brazilian farmers, one unchanging call to repent and turn towards the Father's way of life, one character made new in a thousand languages, one hope seen in a parent's sacrificial love for a child, one victory over death. There is not one expression of faith, one definition of doctrine, one hierarchical system, one organized pattern of Christian life, one set of moral judgments for every eventuality, one liturgy, one insight into the nature of the Trinity. It is precisely the coming together of that 'one' and that 'not one' which makes the Christian journey always fresh and demanding, presenting fresh challenges and bringing new joys. In the period of German mysticism at the beginning of the fourteenth century Johannes Eckhart was preaching about the birth of Christ in the human life by faith. He said: 'There is no stopping place in this life. No, nor was there ever one for any man, no matter how far along the way he's come. This then above all things, be ready for the gifts of God and always for new ones.' It is not altogether surprising that at his death in 1327 Eckhart was under examination for heretical views, and heresy was indeed confirmed later. New gifts, surprises, unexpected challenges to our routine, extraordinary blessings around the next corner, the demolition of old stones, fresh parables, voices hard to interpret, the sloughing of skins of pomp and artificial dignity, the praises of the people of God, these are journey signs. That journey has always been and will always be through a country with no abiding cities but with a single direction, towards the wonder of the light which was brought to us in Jesus.

Change Me

The changeless Christ, with thorns and country eyes,
Is silent, stoic. Pharaoh I recall
Who paces yet, and quite without surprise
Eyes us across his Theban grotto's wall.
Does Christ speak Aramaic still, assured
I'll flit through years to make his language out?
Must we know him as Messianic Lord,
And, without that, live in perpetual doubt?
Would he still call us, each Passover moon,
To take unleavened bread with lamb and wine?
And would he use a modern upper room
To house his guests, who calls the world to dine?
In constant change all living things consist;
Change me, O living Christ; the dead resist.